How to Publish Your

Expert Book

and

Establish Yourself

as the

#1 Choice

In Your Market

(in 30 Days)

Dean Willeford

© 2014 by **Dean Willeford**

All rights reserved. No part of this publication may be reproduced in any form or by any means, including scanning, photocopying, or otherwise without prior written permission of the copyright holder.

First Printing, 2014

Printed in the United States of America

ISBN 13:978-1502491886

ISBN 10:1502491885

Published by

Xpert Publisher
3680 Grant Drive, Suite N
Reno, NV 89509
Expert Publisher.com

Income Disclaimer

This document contains business strategies, marketing methods and other business advice that, regardless of my own results and experience, may not produce the same results (or any results) for you. I make absolutely no guarantee, expressed or implied, that by following the advice below you will make any money or improve current profits, as there are several factors and variables that come into play regarding any given business.

Primarily, results will depend on the nature of the product or business model, the conditions of the marketplace, the experience of the individual, and situations and elements that are beyond your control.

As with any business endeavor, you assume all risk related to investment and money based on your own discretion and at your own potential expense.

Liability Disclaimer

By reading this document, you assume all risks associated with using the advice given, with a full understanding that you, solely, are responsible for anything that may occur as a result of putting this information into action in any way, and regardless of your interpretation of the advice.

You further agree that our company cannot be held responsible in any way for the success or failure of your business as a result of the information presented. It is your responsibility to conduct your own due diligence regarding the safe and successful operation of your business if you intend to apply any of our information in any way to your business operations.

Some links in the book may be affiliate links where the author may receive compensation.

How to Publish Your

Expert Book

and

Establish Yourself

as the

#1 Choice

In Your Market

(in 30 Days)

Dean Willeford

Table of Contents

About the Author..............................13

Introduction......................................15

Chapter 1
Benefits of an Expert Book........19

    Your Ultimate Business Card...... 20
    Ways to Use Your Expert Book... 23
    Credibility.................................... 24
    Career Builder..............................25
    Royalties.......................................26
    Media Exposure........................... 27
    Accomplishment........................... 27
    Authority and Status.................... 28
    Spin Offs......................................28

Chapter 2
Your Market............................31

    Who is Your Market?.....................31
    Lifetime Customer Value...............33
    Your Unique Signature
        Marketing Proposition...............35

Chapter 3
Writing Your Expert Book........43

Target and Theme........................44
Speed Writing..............................44
The Outline................................. 45
The Interview.............................. 46
Transcription................................47
Editing..47

Chapter 4
From Raw Manuscript to Expert Book......................... 49

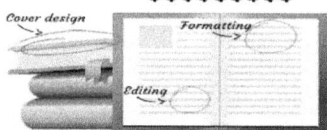

Appearance.....................................50
Title and Sub-Title.......................... 51
Cover and Back Cover....................54
Table of Contents.......................... 56
Look Inside..................................... 56
Price..57
Interior..59
Other Parts.....................................59

Chapter 5
Publishing Your Book...............65

CreateSpace and other
    Print on Demand................66
Create a CreateSpace Account
    From Title to
        Distribution.....................68

Chapter 6
E-Books and Kindle..................85

Format Differences from
    Physical Books.........................86
Conversion with Kinstant..............90
Publishing Your eBook..................90
    Step by Step Instructions

Chapter 7
Marketing Your Expert Book....97

25 Ways to Sell More Books...........98

Chapter 8
Conclusion.............................109

Additional Resources...................... 111
    Books..111
    Consultants............................... 111
    Covers..111
    Cover Design............................ 112
    E-Publishers............................ 112
    ISBN.. 112
    Print on Demand...................... 112
    Publicity......................................112
    Wholesalers............................... 113

Index...114

Notes

Thanks for buying our book.

Please review this book on Amazon.com.

We need your feedback to make the next version better. We want to hear from you. As the reader of this book, you are our most important commentator. We value your feedback.

You can email or write us about what you did or didn't like. We would like to know what areas you would like to see us publish.

When you contact us, please be sure to include the book's title as well as your name and email address.

Email: Consultwithpro@yahoo.com

Mail: Xpert Publisher
Attn: Reader Feedback
3680 Grant Drive, Suite N
Reno, Nevada, 8950

About the Author

Dean Willeford is an Authority Marketing expert, author and speaker whose focus is to show sales professionals, small business owners, entrepreneurs, and professionals how to get more customers, sell more products/services, build a powerful brand and establish themselves as authority leaders in their fields.

He uses referrals, "expert" publications and networking techniques to make you the "Go To" person in your field.

Dean has more than 30 years of marketing, financial and sales experience. He served as CEO of United Publishers, a major yellow pages company, where he brought sales from less than $1 million to over $8 million in less than three years. He has sales experience as a stock broker, mortgage loan broker and sales manager. He is an avid free enterprise activist, and after leaving the corporate world, he founded and built BDS Consulting Group by helping hundreds of small businesses to start, grow and prosper for the last 26 years.

He graduated from University of Southern California (USC) and did graduate work at California State University. At USC he was an All-America swimmer, and later a member of the Olympic team in water polo, and member of the Water polo and Swimming Halls of Fame. Currently he is President of the Nevada Olympians, and is working to bring the Winter Olympics to the Reno-Tahoe area.

Dean is the author of four business books, including *Referrals And..., Cash Out, The iCorporation*, all which can be found on Amazon.com and other outlets.

For more information, Dean's LinkedIn Profile can be founded at www.linkedin.com/in/deangotoexpert/.

If you are serious about growing your business or profession, and want to establish yourself as the number one choice in your market, contact Dean at BDSConsult@gmail.com or call 775-827-1775.

Introduction

What is an "Expert Book"? It is a book you write that displays your expertise, authority and knowledge about your business, practice or profession. Your book creates the perception that you are a step above others in your field. A book can last an entire career; whereas radio, TV, and almost any other form of advertising lasts only a fleeting moment. Advertising has to be paid for again and again to be effective. An original self-written and published book requires some short-term effort, but it continues to promote you and your brand for years, *even an entire career.*

Publishing an Expert Book is relatively simple with modern print on demand and virtual e-book services now available. It is essentially a six-step process:

1. Outlining the book
2. Writing the book quickly
3. Editing
4. Creating the book from a raw manuscript
5. Distribution
6. Marketing

This book shows you how to quickly rip through each step to make you a published expert in your field in 30 to 60 days.

The distribution and marketing steps are where an Expert Book will generally depart from most "traditional" non-fiction works. Since the chief goal of an Expert Book is to establish your credibility, status, expertise and authority, you are less concerned about the number of books you sell for royalties, but are more focused on harvesting clients to become long-term revenue generators for your business.

Selling a book is a limited, one-time event; whereas capturing new clients and customers will bring you multiple revenue-creating events. You are concerned with the long-term value of a customer, not a five-dollar royalty. The new client's value is usually hundreds or thousands of times a one-time book sale.

Even though this book is about writing an Expert Book, it is ultimately about marketing yourself and your business. It is about creating a power platform from which to create great income, expertise, authority, fame and status. For that reason, I have included several topics that relate directly to marketing. You need to know who your target market is, how they can create value for you, how your book will relate to the media and your market and how to sell more copies. Knowing these things will help you to understand how to better use your book to market yourself.

The biggest single factor stopping you from writing your Expert Book is procrastination. When is the last time you thought about writing a book? How many times since then have you sworn you would do it? Did you actually start? How far did you get? Ninety eight out of 100 would-be authors never finish. You start thinking, "I don't know how to publish a book", "I'm afraid to tell my story", "I need to organize my notes to get started", "I get distracted when I try to write". There are always more important or pressing matters that would interfere with your progress. If you have used these excuses in the past, read and follow the suggestions in this Expert Book. You must schedule the time to do it and stick to your schedule.

If you want to be one of the few who do complete their book project, you need a guide, a mentor or coach, a person who will hold you responsible to a schedule of deadlines. With that person, you will be done by the next full moon; without that person, another year will pass. You know this is true. Call me at 775-827-1775 now, and say, "I am ready."

In this book I use the terms "clients", "customers", "patients" and "quests". They are all synonymous. They are anyone who will pay for your product or services.

Your "business" means, a practice, industry, field or profession.

A "prospect" is a potential prospective client, customer, patient or quest.

- So let's get started writing your career changing Expert Book.

Chapter 1

Note to self

Write a book, someday

Benefits of an Expert Book

Writing a book to establish your expertise and authority may be the best career decision you ever make.

A book establishes you as the "go to" person in your industry. You can get royalty payments for every copy sold. A self-published book can be the jumping off point to other related products, such as audiotapes, seminars, paid public speaking, consulting and new paying clients seeking your expertise.

In this new electronic publishing age you can quickly and easily write and publish electronic books, paperback books, and even hardcover books in 30 to 60 days.

This book will show you a quick process that can make you a star, an expert, and a recognized authority in your field. You will stand above the crowd when you can say you have your own books sold on Amazon, Barnes & Noble, iTunes, and 15 other platforms and outlets.

Your Ultimate Business Card

Your book becomes your "ultimate business card". With your name on the front cover you become an instant expert, an authority. To the prospective clients in your field you become *the* recognized authority immediately.

Prospects perceive you as better qualified than others in your field. Your name on the cover completely changes your standing and credibility. You become a leader in your industry.

Your book totally changes your position, leverage, standing and prestige. Because of that, your prospects come to you. You gain the power in the relationship. You don't have to "pitch" your product or services. They tend to ask your opinion and seek your expertise.

When you position yourself correctly, you gain authority. Clients will fall over themselves trying to buy from you, rather than your competitors. You have the power to determine prices, terms, payments, the sales process, referrals and the relationship that you have with them in the future.

For example, price becomes a greatly diminished issue. You can easily charge more, as all specialists do. The conversation or interview centers around the *results* of your product or service, and not on the price.

A similar phenomenon happens when someone refers you. They are 90% sold when they get to you. They deferred to your capabilities and expertise instead of you trying to sell them. A book written by you has the same effect: you become the authority.

When you go to networking events, your business card is only one of many, so there is no reason for them to follow up. But, if you give a good prospect a book, you surprise them, and they will remember you as the stand out. They will spend more time looking at your book than a simple business card. They seldom will throw your book away, it usually goes on their book shelf.

There are many ways to use your book as an introduction to your expertise.

For example, if you are a doctor or dentist and have a book with your name on the cover in the waiting room, imagine the tremendous impact that an authority book has on the prospective client or patient while they are waiting to talk to you. If you personally give it to the prospect after you interview them, you immediately capture their attention. It is an example of your expertise and tremendously increases the value of the interview or consultation with the client or patient. It reinforces hiring you, *rather than someone else* in your field.

You can use your book in many ways to "hook" your prospects. If, for example, you're doing an interview of a prospective client you start by giving a copy or leaving a copy of your book with them. *No one else is doing that.*

You can put many "hooks" in the book, like a link back to your website, where they click to learn more about you. You can use it for list building, where you put a link in and they land on a page where they leave their contact information to be followed up on at a later time.

And you can use your book to get past gatekeepers and assistants to see very important prospects. You can mail the book, or even better still, FedEx the book. It will *always* be opened. I guarantee they'll spend time reading and skimming your book.

For example, you may be an insurance salesman and you try to get to see a very high value client about his estate planning and the use of insurance. You may be talking about a million or $2-3 million policy. These high value prospects are very difficult to gain access to. A book helps smooth the way. They do not spend their time lightly. They want to talk to someone who is professional, knowledgeable and provides solutions to their needs. **Your book is an introduction from one expert to another.**

If you have already given or sent your book to the prospect, you're not just going to be another sales person trying to get in to see him. You are now an expert in using insurance for estate planning services. If you have an appointment, but he does not already have your book, when you come in to see his gatekeeper you might present a business card and a copy of your book as an announcement of your appointment.

If you are a financial planner or stockbroker you could send a copy of your book as a follow-up after your initial introduction or referral. When you make the call to set up an interview or meeting, you can refer back to the book that they received in the mail. Your book introduces you as a true professional and causes a complete change of your status in the eyes of a prospective client.

Real estate agents who have written and published books tell me it is quite common for their closing ratio to more than double. These agents use their book as their "ultimate business card" to leave with prospective listings and sales clients. Type in "real estate sales" at Amazon.com and you will see numerous agents who are using a book as a primary closing device. Most of these agents are very successful and earn well above national norms. If your closing ratio doubles, it can easily mean an additional $10,000 or more in commission on every additional $300,000 house you sell.

Unlike radio, television or print advertising which are gone forever after they are displayed, a book is a marketing piece that lasts for years. So it is well worth the initial time and expense. Typically, one sale or new client will cover the production costs of the book several times over.

Ways to use your book in your marketing

- Use as a pre-introduction to an interview when sending by mail or in person.
  It is very powerful to send a copy after you schedule an appointment, but before you arrive at a presentation. A direct mail delivery will *always* be opened and reviewed.
- Send as a follow-up to an inquiry from other advertising or promotion.
- Use as a follow-up or a "leave behind" after an interview or presentation.
- Customize the title in several ways to further emphasize your expertise.
  1. Put a geo-specific title on the book, Example: *"How to Buy Commercial Property in Dallas, Texas"*.
  2. Use your name in the title. Example: *"Mike Smith's Guide to Hiring a Contractor"*.
- Your book can be used in any way that you currently use a business card, but it has much bigger impact, because it is perceived at a much higher value than a card. You might have a $15-20 price on the cover, even though it only costs you $2.00-2.50.
- Write more than one book on your business, but emphasize a different aspect. Example: Insurance. Your first book might be on life insurance, but the second would be how to use life insurance to save inheritance taxes.
  Much of the same content might be used in both books, thereby making the writing of the second book much easier.
- List your book on your business card and other marketing materials.

- Add a "Purchase my book on Amazon" statement to your website and email list under your email signature.
- Leave it in your waiting room for potential clients to review. Example: In an accountant's office, dentist, cosmetic surgeon, weight loss clinic, etc. It should be one of the few things on the side table.
- You could have custom postal stamps printed that look like your book cover, and put the stamp on every piece of mail you send out. (See Zazzle.com)
- You can put hyperlinks throughout your book that link with one click to your website, your products/services, to a list building page, YouTube videos, etc.
- There are numerous place in your book to enhance your authority and credibility. You can put testimonials and recommendations on the back cover, or in the main content. The "About the Author" page is a perfect place to sell your abilities and put in a call to action by the reader. Put your picture and any awards on the back cover.
- Send the book to your current clients. It almost always generates more business.
- Use your imagination. I'm sure you can think of many more ways that might be specific to your industry.

Credibility

Your name on the cover of a book provides you with instant credibility. Credibility means they believe you, believe what you say and they believe what you show them. The prospect accepts your presentation and you. It implies you have studied and understand your industry better than others in your field since you are an author on the subject.

Your name on a book is like adding another big diploma to your wall. It gives you credentials, and/or another document that provides the base for confidence, belief, authority, and qualifications.

The more you narrow the focus of your book's subject, the more credibility you gain. If you go to a bookstore and find 50 books on the stock market, but your interest is how to trade options, you will select the book about options every time. There is much less competition and fewer books in your category.

To enhance your credibility even further, you have the ability to create a page in your book called "About the Author". This gives you an opportunity to tell the reader not only about the specific subject of this book, but also about other books and articles you have written, organizations you belong to, educational background, and other accomplishments. This is a place where you can "hard sell" yourself without the appearance of "blowing your own horn".

Your published book gives you the opportunity to publish testimonials about your expertise and your good work. You have the ability to put other social proof, like screen captures of your website, or comments on your Facebook page, LinkedIn and others. You could include pictures and images of yourself, your work and events. You can include hyperlinks in your book to your website or any other online sites and data you want to offer your readers.

Career Builder

If you are, or will be a job seeker, how impressive to be able to show a prospective employer that you have written an Expert Book on your job subject. Your book is real physical proof that you have mastered your field. Your book becomes your "enhanced" resume.

Virtually no one is able to present their book at a hiring interview. You will stand out easily. Your chances of getting the job ahead of others will skyrocket.

You can talk about how much more value you bring to the prospective employer as a published author.

As your knowledge and resume expand, you can easily update the book to reflect your increased skills for years into the future.

Royalties

Of course, there are royalties that you can earn for each book you sell. But, you should not expect significant royalties from book sales. Unless you are extraordinarily lucky, you will not be in a league with bestsellers by James Patterson, or Stephen Covey's, *The Seven Habits of Highly Effective People*, or Jack Canfield's *Chicken Soup for the Soul* series of books which have sold millions of copies. Retail success with book sales requires massive marketing.

> - Marketing a book is a completely different enterprise than writing it.

The real purpose of self-publishing a book is to establish your credibility and expertise in your particular field.

As an expert in a particular niche, your niche market probably will be thousands of people, not millions. Your potential readers are generally limited to your market niche.

As a self-published author, your royalties per book can be extraordinarily high compared to a traditional publisher. Royalties and profit margins are usually 40 to 70% of the sales price, whereas in the traditional publishing business you're likely to get 10 to 15%, if you can get a traditional publisher to publish you. Because you are self-publishing, you cut out the middleman.

When you self-publish with Amazon Kindle electronic books, CreateSpace, or others, you have the ability to control your costs and royalties. In the Kindle space you can even give away or lend your books and still receive compensation.

There are many instances where a book only produces a few hundred dollars in royalties, but millions in related products and services.

Media

As a published author you have greater access to free publicity via radio interviews and television appearances. Media are always looking for experts in every field. Once you are known as a source on a particular subject, reporters and media producers will come to you again and again.

Your fame can open many doors to unexpected opportunities to joint ventures and influential people.

Your status as an expert author greatly reduces the risk to radio and television producers who are looking for guests and are therefore more willing to book you as a guest.

If you would like to be cited by the major media and use the mass media logos on your websites, LinkedIn, other social media, business cards, and all other marketing materials, call the author at 775-827-1775 or BDSConsult@gmail.com.

Accomplishment

There is a certain pride in being a published author. Friends, family, acquaintances, business associates, prospects and strangers lend you extra respect and prestige. After all, surveys have found that over 80% of adults say they would like to write a book about their ideas, but only less than 1/4 of 1% do. It is a highly valued badge of accomplishment, perseverance and knowledge. Less than one in a thousand are published author/experts in their field. Your expertise narrows the logical choices in the prospect's mind. After all, why not choose the published expert rather than just another member of the herd?

Most authors have a positive effect on their readers. You can lead the reader to avoid expensive mistakes and encourage them to best practices.

Authority and Status

Your book further enhances your authority in your field. Surround yourself with the trappings of authority and use your book to create greater status as the "go to" person in your field. Feature your book in articles, biographies, sales and promotional materials, websites and social media. In your book, be sure to emphasize your titles, professional designations, board or industry certifications, president or officers of organizations. Includes stories on how your expertise solved the problems that the reader likely has.

Other Product Spin Offs

There are numerous other products and services that you can spin off from a book. You can hyperlink the reader to your websites, where you could have all sorts of products and services to offer them.

For example, if you are a financial planner, you may have numerous insurance products for the reader, become their stockbroker and earn commissions, become a paid consultant on estate planning.

You could create very valuable lists for resale to others who want to reach your kind of customer.

You could create an audio version of the book for people who like to drive and listen instead of reading. Audio products are generally 30 to 50% more expensive than a book and more profitable.

You could create learning or informational courses in audio and video formats and sell them as a package. Once you have written your book, creating audio or video products is really simple.

You could become a paid public speaker as an expert in your field.

If the subject is appropriate, you could create a private label book. This would be a template of your book where another person in your field could put their name on it and use it in a noncompetitive market. For example, if you are in real estate in Dallas, Texas, they could use it in San Diego, California. The other realtor could customize it to their specific market or geographic area by adding pages specific to their market. It would not compete with your book. You might charge $500 to $1,000 for it. They could not list it on Amazon, etc. because it is your copyright and is prohibited in the use contract. They would still have a book about their local market under their authorship.

So, you can clearly see the many benefits of being a published author. Your Expert Book helps you to immediately secure new clients, but also creates your position in the market where customers, clients, and patients want to come to you.

In the next chapter, let's look at who is your market and how a book works to strengthen your presence in that market.

Chapter 2

Your Market

Once you see all the benefits of having your own Expert Book, there are three other considerations to help focus your writing:

1. Determine *specifically* who your audience is.
2. Determine the Lifetime Customer Value (LCV) of the customers or clients you are seeking.
3. What is your Unique Signature Marketing Position (USMP) that causes clients to go to you?

Who is Your Market?

Before you can get into the specifics of writing a book, you need to clearly define your audience. For example, if you are a bankruptcy attorney, the book may be aimed at the general public who are interested in bankruptcy, or it might be aimed at CPAs, other attorneys who can refer business to you, or businesses that are considering bankruptcy. If you are a business attorney, your book might be aimed at a specific business segment, or certain professionals, or small business owners.

If you're a real estate agent, you may want to focus down to a specific geographic area, or a specific real estate segment, such as commercial, just listings, investments, specific kinds of properties like restaurant properties or retail storefronts, etc. If you are a real estate agent in Beverly Hills, you are much more likely to get a listing in Beverly Hills than if you are just an agent in Southern California.

To help you focus your writing, create an avatar of your ideal reader. Write down specifically who your audience is. Consider their demographics, their geographies, and their psychographics.

Where do they live? What state, region, city, town? Are they near the ocean, mountains, desert, rich neighborhoods, or snow country?

What are their ages, hobbies, interests, income levels? Are they male, female, short tall, thin, or fat? Are they business owners, employers, management, blue collar, investors, homeowners, condo dwellers? Are they single, married, have children, etc.?

Are they healthy, sick, looking for relationships, gay, straight?

The avatar might look like this:

My readers are middle aged, female career women, who lives in a city in the south. They makes $70,000 to $100,000 per year and is self-employed, working 50-60 hours per week. She is once divorced with no children. She is a little overweight and eats out a lot, etc.

Considering these things will make your book more focused and it will be easier to create the title, the cover, stories or examples to use, and how you will market to them.

This step is easy to do and helps you pinpoint your market, your writing theme or point of view.

Lifetime Customer Value (LCV)

Even though this book is about writing a book, it is equally important to understand the significance of acquiring that *initial* client, customer or patient. Your Expert Book is aims at acquiring AND retaining the customer or clients. Your book gives you the opportunity to cement your expertise and value for the long term, not just the initial sale.

The Lifetime Customer Value (LCV) is the amount of the first sale, plus a lifetime of purchases from your customers, plus the dollar value of the purchases of the people who are referred to you.

Your goal as a business professional is not to just make a one-time sale to a customer and forget about them. Your goal is to have your customers come back to you over and over, to buy from you as many times as possible, and buy as much of your product line as possible.

Whether you own a corner market, or are an auto mechanic, restaurateur, salesperson, doctor, dentist or lawyer, it is imperative you get repeat and continuing business from your clients/customers to be successful.

Your best customer is your current customer; they already know and trust you. Your current customers are your most profitable customers and it costs very little to retain them, as compared to acquiring new clients and customers. Many studies have shown it costs seven times more to gain a new customer than to keep an old one. So, once you get a customer, do everything you can to retain them.

The classic example is an accountant. The accountant may do a client's tax return once per year for $200, but he has the potential to create additional revenue from monthly bookkeeping work, weekly payroll preparation, and quarterly payroll tax returns. He can offer preparation of numerous kinds of local reports and taxes, like business taxes, business licenses, sales taxes, excise taxes, loan document preparation, business plans, other form of consultation and the referrals that the client gives along the way.

That $200 tax return could easily turn into a client worth $5,000-$10,000 or more per year. Since clients typically stay with their accountant for many years, that client could easily be worth $100,000 in the LCV.

The accountant example seems obvious, but every business owner and professional has similar products and service line extensions to offer that customer who already knows and trusts them.

A new book written by you and sent to your current customers will almost always produce additional business. You will be surprised by the number of current customers who do not know about the other products and services you currently offer.

To look at it from the reverse side, can you imagine a restaurant succeeding without recurring customers? It would just not be possible.

Marketing surveys have shown businesses lose customers for the following reasons:

- 1% die
- 3% move away
- 5% because of other relationship (relatives, etc.)
- 9% leave for competitive reasons
- 14% leave because of product dissatisfaction
- 68% stop buying your product or service because of an attitude or feeling of indifference

Clearly, the last three reasons (totaling 91%) you can do something about.

How to stimulate business from your current customers? Treat them well and communicate with them often. Gather your customers' names and contact information at every opportunity. My book, Referrals And...shows dozens of ways to use your current customers to get referrals and endorsements.

Communicate with your customer list regularly, by postcard, fax, email, Twitter, telephone, and letter. There are automated systems that can handle this communication for very small expense compared to its value. The value of an unused customers' list depreciates at the rate of over 10% a month.

When you cultivate your customers' list no-cost referrals become common, and the referral is 90% sold when they come to see you. Your customers, clients and patients buy more, and more frequently. If you do this right, you can cut down on other advertising costs to pay for this communication. You can give away copies of your book like business cards to people who are referral sources. Your competitors are always trying to get your customers. Create an unbreakable bond with your clients; do not take your current customers for granted.

One of the most important bonds becomes your personalized Expert Book(s) in their home or business

Unique Signature Marketing Position (USMP)

When you write a book it is critically important to present the reason customers, clients and patients should come to you *above all others* in your industry. This will make your book much more powerful.

When you know your Unique Signature Marketing Position (USMP) it creates a clear laser-focused message in your book.

- **The USMP message is the reason people will buy from you.**

The USMP is the unique message to your prospective customers that will set your business above all the other "me too" companies in your industry and in your market. It is a simple concise statement of benefit that makes you unique.

There are many ways to characterize the USMP:

1. It is the idea that sets you apart from every other competitor in your business.
2. The USMP makes customers say to themselves, "I would have to be crazy to do business with anyone else". Many times, it is regardless of the price.
3. It leads people to think you're the only logical choice.
4. Your USMP creates the most value in your customer's mind.
5. Your USMP is the singular, unique benefit that your customers can expect to receive when they buy from you instead of your competitors.

Most businesses are "me too" businesses. Your ultimate business success is determined by the unique value you bring to your customers. If you have no unique values, customers have no reason to use your business over all others in your category.

Just look at the yellow pages for "me too" businesses. Pick a category. Let's say, movers. They all claim the same thing: faster service, credit cards accepted, the lowest prices, careful, long pattern business, friendly service, commercial and residential, etc. They all say the same thing - no reason to pick one over the other.

So, how do the customers decide? Since they are all the same, they compare prices. That's why price becomes so important in the customer's mind. But, more on price later.

When you create a unique reason for people to use you, you must be able to deliver all your USMP promises. If you don't deliver, the word gets around very quickly, and prospective customers will avoid your business or they will never return.

Most businesses have no USMP, and that is why 80% of all businesses fail within the first five years, and 51% in the first year. There's no particular reason to do business with them. They survived by the sheer number of people who need a product or service, or until their money runs out. This is clearly seen in new high growth industries, where demand is so great for the new service that the customers will do business with anyone, at first.

Computers were a good example. There were hundreds of computer makers in the beginning when everyone was a potential customer. As the market became saturated, people began to look for unique features and benefits instead of just the "me too" product. They began to look for something that would provide extra value to their purchase. Since most had no unique, compelling or extra value in their product, they began to lose customers. Soon the field was narrowed to those who brought extra value and benefits to the table. Now there are only a handful of computer makers.

A USMP is clear, concise, simple, and specific. Here are some examples:

1. The Uncola ™
2. Absolutely, positively overnight™
3. Three Day Blinds™
4. Fresh hot pizza delivered in 30 minutes or less, guaranteed
5. The 99¢ Store™
6. Ruffles have Ridges™

These USMP messages become so valuable they are trademarked.

- **Each USMP carries a unique message about the benefit the customer wants**.

There are unlimited possibilities for creating your USMP. The best ones are where there is a void or weakness in your industry, but that's not absolutely necessary.

USMP can be speed, convenience, location, delivery, quality, variety, taste, colors, fun, snob appeal, exclusivity, rarity, hours of operation, financing, expertise, design, reliability, price, guarantees, specialization and dozens of others which may be unique to your industry.

One more word about price.

All customers want the same thing: **the best deal.** But price is not the real issue. It's the value they receive that is the determining factor in purchasing. Most of the time they will place more value on the USMP than price. Think about it. Do you always buy the cheapest?

There's no real reason to compete on price when there are dozens of other ways to do it. Price competition has a very negative influence on profitability. Price competition hurts your ability to provide more value added services and textures. Lower prices hurt quality. Price shoppers are not loyal, and have more problems and more returns.

Look at all the giants that ignore price and provide another USMP.

1. **7-11 Stores** are 30% more expensive than the local supermarket. Why can they charge more? **Convenience**. Fast in and out. They carry many of the same products, but people are willing to pay extra for their USMP.
2. **Deluxe Checks Corporation** charges 100-150% more for the same product ordered independently instead of through your bank. Why? **Convenience**. All you do is choose the color and style the first time and check a box to reorder. The company even has enough profit to pay a commission to the banks on each fulfilled order.

3. **Lens Crafters** cost 40% to 70% more for the **speed** of the delivery. They built an entire giant company on delivery of your glasses in 1 to 2 hours, instead of two or three days as used to be the norm. Now it has become almost the standard in the industry.
4. **Rolex Watches** cost $2,000 to $10,000 without precious stones. You can buy a watch that keeps perfect time for $10.00. Why would you pay more? Rolex have sold you on their USMP: **Prestige and Quality**.
5. **Apple Computers** are 30-40% more than PCs, yet they have built a loyal following because of their USMP- **design and ease of use.**

These are all well-known names of large companies, but the same concept worked equally well in local markets. Many times a good USMP works even better because you're not competing with giants with unlimited money and marketing expertise.

The whole concept of USMP rarity and specialization reinforces your position. For example, there are lots of doctors, all have M.D. after their name, but few have the board specialty after their name. The board specialty makes the doctor more valuable, prestigious, and carries more authority. Still fewer have a sub-specialty, again adding to their worth even more. And finally, how many of those doctors have written a book on their specialty, therefore making them the ultimate "go to" person in their field?

If a business is looking for a new location for a manufacturing plant, are they going to the real estate agent who sold the owner his home? Probably not. They will go to a commercial realtor because that realtor has more authority, expertise and knowledge of that particular market.

There are lots of diamonds, but at each step in their clarity, color and size their price increases exponentially. Each step you take in defining your expertise and authority further enhances your value. Your Expert Book is a written statement of your increased value.

The very act of creating a USMP and specializing within your field labels you as an expert in that area. Your specialization enables you to charge more for your skills and knowledge. An accountant is a perfect example of how this hierarchy works. The accountant has a high school degree, a college degree, a state's certificate designating him as Certified Public Accountant (CPA) for his accounting knowledge. Each step along the way increases his value and expertise. When the CPA writes a book on his specialized subject, it gives him an additional step up above even other CPSs in his field.

When you focus your practice or business on a specific area, be sure to let all the colleagues in your field know what you are doing. Inevitably many of those colleagues will defer to your specialized expertise and send you referrals. Your competitors actually can be a great source of business.

I know a bankruptcy attorney who specializes in Chapter 11 business bankruptcy reorganizations. Many other attorneys in his area who handle standard, simple Chapter 7 and 13 cases, send him the more difficult and profitable Chapter 11 cases.

The same concept works for realtors, dentists, accountants, attorneys, specialty contractors and so on. Each step along the way adds value.

Create a USMP in your book that sets you apart and above all the others in your field and geographic market.

Once you have made up your mind on the specific market segment, the outline in your writing process becomes immeasurably easier.

Now that we have shown you the benefits of being a published author and how that strengthens your position in your market place. The next chapter shows you how to get past the biggest roadblock in the book writing process. It is a system to write your book in as little as a weekend. You can use the system alone or with the help of another person. We recommend you enlist another person to quickly move forward. Remember, procrastination is the biggest enemy of creating a book.

Chapter 3

Writing Your Expert Book

One of the keys to writing your Expert Book is to do it as quickly as possible. Get it down on paper without editing. This is important because it gets the basic ideas in writing. After you have the rough manuscript, you refine and edit it paragraph by paragraph. As you begin the editing process you will not only make corrections and clarifications, but also you will inevitably add and subtract from the content. You will add stories, proof, examples and evidence to your basic ideas.

Naturally, most people think writing the book is the most difficult part of the process. In fact it is the easiest to do, especially for "experts", because they already have the knowledge in their heads. They just need to get it down on paper.

Target and Theme

Before you begin outlining and writing, you can take two steps that will make your writing much easier.

The first is to clearly identify your target audience. If you are an attorney writing to other attorneys, your style and vocabulary are going to be different than writing for the general public. Refer back to the avatar we suggested you create earlier. Write down on a 3x5 card exactly who your intended reader is. The act of writing it will help you focus.

Secondly, write down your theme, angle, point of view or what makes your book different from other books on the same subject. Take a position, express a definite opinion about your subject. Express pet peeves or bias. Lead the reader to your position.

These two steps alone will determine how you will answer a great number of the interview questions at the heart of your book.

Speed Writing

If you follow this simple speed writing strategy you can have your basic book written in a matter of days or a weekend. The actual publishing will take a bit more time

Step One: Outline

This should only take 30 to 45 minutes. Take a piece of paper and write down the 12 most frequently asked questions (FAQ) that your

clients/customers have, in question form. The author of this book also uses a 50 question generic interview form to stimulate discussion of your subject, and questions clients should ask.

Buy a pack of two hundred 3x5 cards. Write one of those FAQ questions on each card. These will become book chapters.

Now, delete at least one of the main question cards, usually the least important or the one that you feel does not belong. This helps you tighten and focus the book.

After that, get 10-12 additional blank cards for each of the main questions. On these cards write subtopics about the main chapter question. Turn over the card and write one to three words or phrases that are reminders of what to talk about on that card. Do this for each of the FAQs.

Now, do the above process for the "should asked questions". These are the questions that customers don't have enough knowledge to ask. They tend to be follow-up questions from the original questions.

Do not number the cards, because you may want to re-arrange the cards for idea flow and logical progression.

Or alternatively, if your book is a "list" book like *"The 34 Sources of Tax Free Income"*, write one item of your list on each card and a few words on the back to remind you about the points you want to cover.

After you have all your cards completed, organize them in order of importance and priority. Now you have the 10-11 main questions, a few subtopics for each chapter/question, the 10 "should asked" questions and finally a few words as talking points about each. Now, you will have a good overview of your subject.

In less than one hour you will have the outline for your book.

Step Two: Interview

Set up a microphone and an audio recorder (or a computer with audio recording voice recognition software) at a table. You can buy a good microphone or digital recorder and voice recognition software for less than $100.

Sit down with another person and have them "interview" you. The person will use the cards you have prepared to ask you questions. You use the subtopic cards to refer to so you can stay focused on that subject. The person may also ask additional questions based on your recorded answers. This will help clarify your answers and make them more understandable for the eventual reader. This is very similar to making a presentation and answering questions from a prospective customer.

This will be easy because the answers are already in your head. You are the expert. You can look up specific numbers, names, examples or citations to fill in the blanks after you get the basics on paper. You just need to get the whole "interview" down on paper.

This may take more than one session, but in a couple of hours each, you will have a raw manuscript of 110 plus pages. When you add additional examples and stories it will expand your book further.

Step Three: Transcription

After you have gone through all the cards, have the interview transcribed into a raw manuscript. A transcriber will cost $30 to $50 per hour, or you can do it yourself. If you use Microsoft voice recognition or

Dragon voice recognition software, most of the transcription work will be done.

You can have a raw manuscript in six to ten hours depending on your subject or on the number of "chapters" on your cards.

Step Four: Editing

Now you will begin the editing process and structuring the book for maximum impact. Editing includes polishing up the grammar, phrasing language, spelling and clarifying, deleting and adding ideas.

It is important to bring in a third party to edit your book. You can do an initial edit, but you are simply too close to your work to see its flaws.

Ask our editor to address these areas:

- Clarity of ideas.
- Rewriting content to improve idea flow.
- Correcting grammar and spelling.
- Typographical errors.
- Fact checking.

You can hire a professional editor for $20 to $40 per hour for 5-10 pages per hour.

After you have a raw manuscript, you begin structuring the book. This has to do with adding items that make the book more readable and interesting. It includes transition paragraphs from one subject or chapter to the next. It includes adding stories and examples of your main points.

You will include "call to action" items that encourage the reader to do something. You may want to include images, charts, or pictures.

You may put in hyperlinks to your website, resources, landing pages to collect names for a list. We will talk about each of these structuring features in the following chapters.

- The editing process will take more time than any other step. This is where you create a book from a raw manuscript. There will be a number of times the book will be changed, corrected and refined before it is finally offered to your market.

Chapter 4

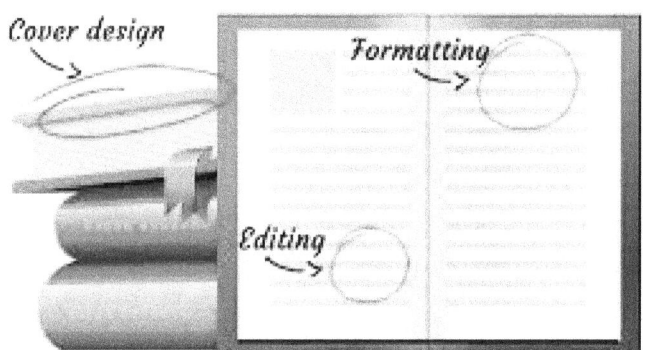

Creating Your Expert Book from a Raw Manuscript

Now you are in the book creation process. While you are doing that, there is a long list of individual items that you will need to add to actually create a physical book or e-book.

You will need to:

- Create a cover and back cover.
- Create title and subtitle.
- Write a Table of Contents.

- Get a "head shot" photograph for the "About the Author" page or back cover.
- Write a biographical sketch for your "About the Author" page.
- The disclaimer page.
- Gather appropriate images or pictures for the book's interior.
- Write a compelling introduction.
- Write a "Call to action" and request for reviews page.
- Create any videos, landing pages, or websites to send readers to.
- Copyright the book.
- Obtain an ISBN number.
- Obtain a Bar Code.
- Advance Information Form (ABI) from Bokker for Books in Print listing.
- Gather testimonials and other social proof to include.
- Write a compelling description for Amazon or other distributors.

- Your publisher will help you create all the above to make your manuscript a book.

Appearance

How your book looks is important to its appeal. First impressions mean a lot, just like when you meet people for the first time. They draw immediate conclusions and tend to make judgments about the content or substance of your book.

Publishers' studies show that readers look at a number of the following book elements in this order of importance:

- Title and subtitle
- Cover
- Back cover

- Flaps or jackets
- Table of Contents
- First few paragraphs
- Price

If you are a celebrity or famous author, then your name and picture become important, otherwise the title and subtitle carry more weight.

Each of the above is of a little less importance in an Expert Book because you are not as concerned about the shelf appeal, but more about establishing your expertise and authority. But still, that first impression is important to judge you favorably.

Title and Subtitle

A title can make or break a book. There are many components that go into the making a strong title. The title words should be short, emotionally charged, action oriented, alliterative and even provocative. But, most of all, they should clearly state what the books is about. It does not hurt if it reads read like a newspaper's headline. Magazines and newspapers are masters at attracting attention in short phrases. Be specific. The title should be aimed at highly targeted audiences and offer clear solutions.

The title should do one or more things:

Make or imply a benefit or promise:

- The One Minute Manager
- The 4-Hour Workweek
- No More Cold Calls

Identify a need or desire:

- The Total Money Makeover
- The Woman's Guide to............
- Endless Referrals

State the content:

- Biographies
- Black's Law Dictionary

How to do something:

- How to ....in 5 Easy Steps, or .... in 20 Minutes or Less
- How to Pay Zero Taxes
- How to Make Friends and Influence People

The subtitle completes the title and tells the whole story. The subtitle should offer benefits and an explanation of the contents.

You might customize the book's title to a geographic area or specific sub-industry.

For example," The Guide to Selling Retail Properties in Southern California"

Try to work key words into your title and subtitle. Look at Google Key Words for words that relate to your subject. This will make the book more appealing to internet searches. Look at Amazon.com and U.S. Trademark searches to eliminate duplicate titles. Pull up a domain search at GoDaddy.com for good domain names that would work well with your title.

Be sure the URL is available (or something very close) for your main title. Try to use a .com, not .net, .co. info, etc. Do an online search to be sure your title is not already taken, or if there is a proprietary name or trademark.

The title can make the difference between selling a few copies or thousands of copies. For example, there was a book published in the 1980s called, *"Astrological Love"*,by Naura Hayden. It sold a few hundred copies. But, an enterprising marketer bought the right to re-publish it under the title, *"How to Satisfy a Woman Every Time ...and Have Her Beg for More"*. It sold 2.5 million copies. *It had the same content inside.*

- Title is extremely important.

Although your goal is to establish your expertise and authority, it would not hurt to sell more copies and motivate your prospects to read it.

Start by writing down on a 3x5 card each title that pops into your mind. In addition to individual titles on the 3x5 cards, create a separate sheet and make a list of words that relate to your topic. Don't prejudge, just write them.

This is where knowing your avatar helps. Go to Amazon Key Words search and type in key words that relate to your subject. Look at titles of other books in your genre. Eliminate the titles that are already taken.

Think of words that would appeal to readers in your subject. Add adverbs, adjectives, action and power words. Begin playing with the words and phrases by combining them. Freely associate the words and phrases. If you can do this with several other supportive people, all the better. More ideas will flow and you will get a better sense of the word's impact by bouncing them off the others.

Try to make your title speak to the results or benefit for your specific audience. Does it communicate instantly with your specific audience? Stay away from general descriptions. Instead of *"The Bike Manual"* try, *"The Bike Racers' Winner's Bible"*. You get the picture.

Come up with a minimum of 10 titles and begin to test them on others. Let them brew in your head while you finish your writing and editing.

Cover

The cover is simply retail packaging. Like any other product it should state what's in for the intended audience.

The cover is just as important as what is in your book, because the cover can greatly motivate the prospective reader to open it. If they don't open it, it doesn't matter much what is inside.

Good design is the essence of the cover. It should not detract from the title. It should be easy to read. Obviously, the cover should be appropriate for the subject, with images or type styles that are suggestive of the content.

The cover color should be appropriate to the book's subject. You should use contrasting colors where the font style is easy to read and will stand out from others on a bookshelf. If they can't read it, they probably won't open it.

The cover not only acts as protection for the book pages, but more importantly, it becomes your number one sales device.

If you are going to publish and sell your book on Amazon, you must be aware of the size limitation when your title is displayed, they use a postage stamp size image of your cover. Here are two examples. Which one is easier to read? The title must be big, bold and easy to read in this small size. The cover images

should not drown out or distract from your title text. Use contrasting colors that don't blend in.

Cover images are about marketing and selling, so good design is a must. Images of people should be attractive. Both men and women like to look at attractive women. Take a lesson from magazine covers.

You can create a cover using several software programs (see the resource section). Amazon.com/CreateSpace have an adequate cover creator (see next chapter). There are many competent cover designers available at Elance.com, Fiver.com, etc.

Back Cover

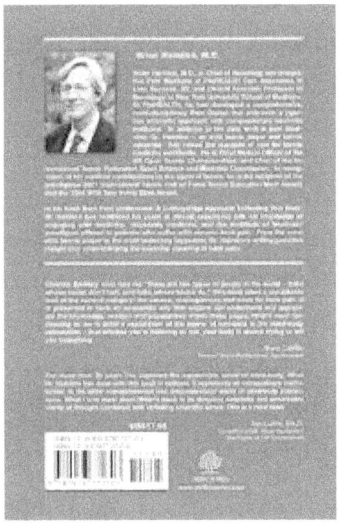

The back cover should further motivate the reader to open the book. The back cover gives you the opportunity to summarize the contents, a place for quick testimonials, to show the author's picture, a brief biography, a summary of benefits and features in a bullet point format.

The back cover is a great place to tell the reader why you are an expert. Create a call to action to buy, call you, go to a website or to take any action you want.

Finally, be sure to include the price, the ISBN number, bar code and the publisher's information.

Flaps and jackets serve the same purpose as back covers

Part of the cover includes a spine. Try to make your title as large and striking as possible, and include a logo if you have one. On a book shelf, the spine is all the prospective reader will see.

Table of Contents (TOC)

The TOC is a summary of the main points of the book. The chapter headings should answer the question, "what's in it for me". The chapters need to imply benefits and offer solutions. Many times one chapter will speak to a specific interest a reader has, and tip the buying decision.

To make the reading more interesting, you may want to word your chapters as questions. For example, a dentist's book might have a chapter called, "Tooth Sensitivity". Instead call it, "What Makes Your Teeth Hurt?" It is more provocative and begs the answer. Questions are a good way to title your chapters.

Regardless of how you title your chapters, be clear what the chapter is about. Don't use a heading that will only be discovered after you read it.; it does not invite the reader to open it and is annoying. I have seen many books where the chapter headings give no clue as to the content.

In an e-book, make the chapters clickable. It makes the book much more reader friendly. (We will discuss more about how to set-up the TOC in a later chapter.)

There are several ways to set up the TOC. Kindle book formatting can easily distort a manually set up TOC because they are viewed on so many different sized screens, many with very limited space. As you can imagine, e-books look much different on smart cell phones than a full-sized iPad or desktop.

The First Few Paragraphs

The first few paragraphs give the reader a sense of how the language of a book flows. Is it easy to read? Is it visually appealing? This is the chief reason Amazon Kindle books have the "Look Inside" feature on the page that has the book description and cover view. This feature is supposed to duplicate the bookstore browsing experience where you can get a brief idea of how the book reads. You may want to put in a clickable link to your website in that first 10% of the book.

Price

Definitely put a price on your Expert Book. Price is normally not very important, especially for an Expert type book. A person will pay $3.00 or $5.00 more if it solves a problem or creates an opportunity. Most of the time you will probably be giving it away, as a gift, an introduction, a premium, or a hook.

A higher price for your Expert Book may even be a benefit; it will be perceived as having more value to your potential audience. A gift of $20 is certainly more respected than one for $2.00. If the prospect buys the book, you could offer to reimburse the cost if they become a client, or give a special discount code for special prospects.

If you create an electronic book on Kindle, you will probably have a lower price to take into consideration because there is no physical book. When you create a Kindle account, one of the sections that you will encounter is how you will price your book. Pricing also affects royalty payments.

There are two royalty options from CreateSpace (and unlimited if you publish on a vanity press):

1. 35% royalty, or

2. 70% royalty.

To qualify for the 70% royalty, you need to meet the two following criteria:

- The work has to be an original work; that is, it cannot be public domain material. Since this is a book about your expertise, this will not come into play.

- You must sell the book for between $2.99 and $9.99.

Of course you're asking yourself, "Why would I take the lower royalty bracket?"

There are three reasons someone would choose the 35% bracket:

1. Publishing public domain works. This is not your concern.
2. Lead generation. These people want to sell the book for the lowest prices possible for the purpose of generating leads for other products and services. The minimum price is 99¢.
3. For people who want to publish premium products. If you price your book for more than $9.99 you can only select the 35% royalty option. You could go for as high as $199 on Amazon.

If you sell your book with other "print on demand" companies, you have much more flexibility on price. You can price your book as you please. If you sell through CreateSpace e-store you receive 80% royalty *after* you pay the book's production costs.

CreateSpace has a royalty calculator that takes into consideration the number of pages and size of your book to determine the royalty after all costs you pay.

If you make your sale through Amazon's website you earn a royalty of 60% of the cover price minus the production costs. If the sales are made through an expanded distribution network you receive 40% of the cover price minus the production costs.

Of course, if you order copies as the author, there's no royalty paid, but you get the books at the production cost plus shipping.

The major attraction of the print on demand companies is that you can print very small quantities if you wish. That way, you do not have an inventory of books you pay for that are sitting around waiting for distribution.

Interior

For the interior of your book the text size should be 12 or 14 point font. Use a simple font style like Georgia or New Roman Times, unless the book's subject calls for a specific theme. For example, a children's book will probably call for more images, color and a more playful and larger font style.

Other Book Parts

There are a number of other parts of the book that you need to create that are not necessarily about appearance. You will need to create all of the following:

Title Page

The title page includes a title, the subtitle, the author's copyright, the publisher and contact information. On the next page, tell the reader, "All rights are reserved. No part of this publication may be been reproduced in any form, or by any means without prior written permission of the copyright holder."

This page also usually includes the ISBN numbers. Sometimes there is acknowledgement for cover design and illustrations.

About the Author Page

This page is especially important for an Expert Book. This is the place for a blatant sales pitch about yourself. Create a biographical sketch that relates to your expertise and credibility. If you have credentials, diplomas, specialty training and licenses that enhance your credibility, mention them here. Borrow additional credibility from the schools, universities, companies and organizations that you have been associated with. Include any books, articles, reports you may have written, and media appearances and interviews

Review the Book Page

This will help sales at Amazon and other outlets. Reviews give you the opportunity to find out what your potential customers and clients are interested in.

Thank them for buying the book and ask the reader for a review. If your book is on Amazon or other electronic platforms, ask them to review it there. Reviews are extremely important on Amazon. Readers lend a great deal of credibility to those reviews. Also include an email address where they can write to tell you their comments.

Disclaimer Liability Page

Even if you are a lawyer, accountant or doctor, you don't want to be giving legal, accounting or medical advice, because everyone's situation and circumstances are different. Make it clear that the book is either legal, accounting or medical advice.

Be sure readers know that by reading your book, they assume all risk associated with using the information therein. Readers are responsible for anything that may occur as a result of putting the information into action. Results will depend on many factors outside your control.

The reader is responsible for their own due diligence about the information in your book.

Structure

Structure is the process of adding elements that make the book more interesting and marketable. For example, at the end of each chapter, you might add a paragraph to lead the reader into the next chapter. Create curiosity about what comes next. Leave them hanging so the reader does not want to put it down. Novelists are masters of this technique.

This gives you the opportunity to add stories and examples of points you make in the book. People love stories, they illustrate the points. People relate to them and make them recall being "in their shoes". Images, charts or graphs make the book more appealing and easier to read and understand.

Introduction/ Forward

The introduction section come after the Table of Contents and then resells the reader on why they bought the book and what to expect.

You could include how and why you wrote the book, and what it is trying to accomplish. Tell the reader what they will get out of it. Acknowledge your intended audience and why you think the topic is of interest to them. You may have a brief description or overview of the total book.

You might have any special definitions of words and phrases that are out of the ordinary or beyond their usual usage.

If the book has a special structure, describe how it should be used and for what purpose.

This also is a good place to talk about the author's credibility and experience.

You could include a list of people to acknowledge and a brief reason why.

Call to Action

Tell the reader to do something that you want to happen. It may be to contact you, so be sure to include your contact information. You may want the reader to go to your website, call for an appointment or free consultation. Ask the reader to go to a link to sign up for a newsletter, a check list or other materials. This gives you the opportunity to build a list of interested parties to contact later. You may even ask them to buy something.

Warn against waiting. Tell the reader what they will lose if they procrastinate.

Not only call for the action in the introduction, but also sprinkle in links to yourself, company or product.

Additional Resources or References

If you have additional resources, such as software, books, seminars or other learning materials, prepare that list for inclusion at the end of the book. Obviously, you may want to have any other materials or books that you have written mentioned in this section.

Copyright

It is not absolutely necessary that you copyright your book, although most authors feel a greater sense of security if they do. The copyright is a form of protection provided by the laws of the United States to the authors of "all original authorship". This includes not only books but other works of art, music, etc. This protection is available to both published and unpublished works. Section 106 of the 1976 Copyright Act generally gives the holder of the copyright the exclusive right to authorize others to:

- Reproduce the work by copying or audio reproduction.
- Distribute copies for sale or transfer ownership.
- Perform the work publicly.
- Display the work publicly.

It is illegal for anyone to violate any rights provided to the owner of the copyright by the copyright law. There are some exceptions, the major one being the "fair use" doctrine, which allows for quoting from the work in other limited uses. For an overview of the U.S. copyright law go to U.S. Copyright com.

There are three ways to copyright your book.

The first way is known as a "poor man's copyright". You simply make a copy of your book and mail it to yourself. When you get it, do not open it. The postmark serves as written proof of its existence at that date. If there is a question as to the creation date, you have proof. This method is not 100% foolproof, but it is inexpensive.

A second method is to hire a copyright attorney, and let the attorney handle all the details.

The third method is to use an online service like Legal Zoom.com. Simply go to their site, go to the copyright section and follow their simple instructions. Their fee is in the $125-150 range.

Book Description

One of the steps you'll encounter in the CreateSpace setup process is to create a book description. This is what will initially appear on Amazon's website. Shortly thereafter, you may go to Author Central to update the description and provide a more provocative and interesting description.

On this page, after the description, you'll be asked to provide basic information about your book. Fill in the appropriate fields.

One of the very important fields is key word search. Put in as many relevant key words to your title and subject as possible. This will help readers find your book among the numerous choices they will have in your field.

Index

An index does the same thing as a table of contents, but is more detailed and placed at the end of the book. It is organized by topic or keyword. An index makes your book much more reader friendly and easier to use. An index is also a helpful sales tool, in that many readers look at an index to see if the book covers topics they are interested in.

Chapter 5

Publishing Your Book.

Now you should have a finished manuscript, a cover, title, the description, key words and other book elements we discussed in the previous chapter. You should have saved your manuscript as a Microsoft Word document and in Adobe PDF format. You should have these things ready because it will greatly speed up the publishing process. You will be ready to cut and paste instead of stopping to create them.

But, it is not yet in a format that can be published as an e-book on Kindle or a physical book on CreateSpace.

Although there are many book publishers and printers, we're going to discuss the premier self-publisher, Amazon CreateSpace, because in this author's opinion, it is the simplest to use and offer the greatest value. They also have more than 50% of the self-publishing and e-book market. As an additional benefit of the Amazon package, it provides the author with a place to display and sell your book with a minimum of hassle. Amazon handles all the purchasing, delivery, and distribution.

CreateSpace

As far as this author is concerned, the only way to create a physical book is through CreateSpace.com, an Amazon company. For self-published authors, it offers just too many advantages to ignore.

Let's look at the CreateSpace format first, which allows you to print your book on demand. The advantage of print on demand is that it allows you to create as few or as many copies of the book as you wish. You can have the book delivered into your hands in as few as two days.

This process allows you to purchase copies of the book for personal distribution, and still keep a profit margin of 40% to 80% of your list price. All you have to do is deduct the production costs for each book. The production costs vary depending on the size, and number of pages and whether it's in color or black and white. There is a handy production cost estimator in your account.

You can get an electronic proof copy or a physical copy before you begin to sell it. You can sell your book directly through CreateSpace e-store or you can list it in the Amazon marketplace.

One of the other good reasons to use CreateSpace is that they take care of bothersome details. You can get a 13-digit International Standard Book Number (ISBN) number through CreateSpace, instead of paying for it through R.R. Bowker. The number is a unique number that is assigned to every book. It identifies the publisher and your product as a specific version of a specific title.

CreateSpace also assigns your book a Bar Code. This is the book's ISBN and a price code in retail store scanner format. Retailers and wholesalers insist on the code to ring up transactions. Again, CreateSpace saves you money.

One of the steps that you or your publisher should take is to complete an Advanced Book Information (ABI) form. The ABI form gets the book into R.R. Bowker's *Books in Print*, the publishing industry's bible. Everyone in the trade uses *Books in Print* as *the* source of information on titles and publishers. You can register your book online at http://www.bowkerlink.com website under "Books in Print". Do this as soon as possible, because it can take up to three months to appear.

- The balance of this chapter will be easier to follow if you visit Createspace.com.

Create a CreateSpace Account

Go to http://www.createspace.com. to create an account.

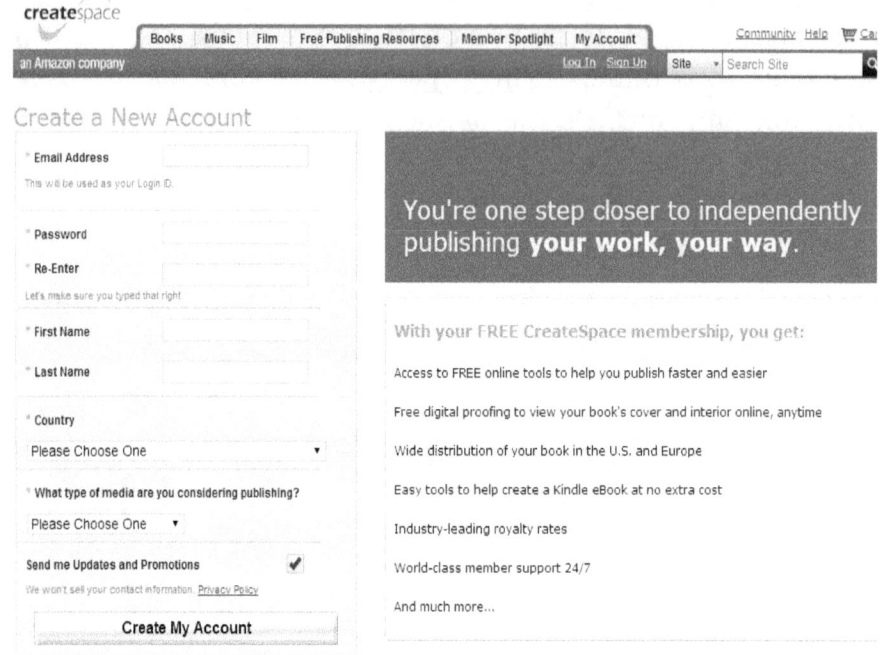

Creating an account is fairly straightforward. It is free and easy to do. The account gives you access to all the tools to publish your book. It includes a free digital proofing tool so you can see what your book will look like before you publish and distribute.

Provide the email address and create a password. Use your real name. If you want to use a pen name you can use it later in the process. Tell them what kind of product you are creating, because they also create other kinds of media.

Press the "Create My Account" button and read the member's agreement and accept it.

Confirm your email by the link CreateSpace will send you.

Account Set-up

You are given two options; one is "Do It Yourself", the other invites CreateSpace to do it for you. Needless to say, the second option will cost you. The process is clear enough that almost anyone can do it themselves. Skip the "other option".

Continue to the link at the bottom that says "Continue to your Member Dashboard". Click on the Alert and message and clear them. You will get two default messages that say "Welcome". Click the "Start fixing the issue" link. That will bring you to the Account Set-up page where you begin putting in Account Settings.

The first one is "Royalty Payment Profile". Since you want royalties, complete the information. The address should be where you pay your taxes. At the end of the year Amazon will send you IRS Form 1099 tax information as to how much you have earned during the year. This information also goes to the federal government.

You may receive your royalty payments via direct deposit to a bank account or a check in the mail. Fill out the payment information and read the country information. There is a $100 minimum before they will send a paper check.

If you have a company, read and fill out the company information and your tax identification number. If you are an individual, use your name and social security number.

If you do not provide the proper information, Amazon will withhold 30% of your royalties and later submit them to the government.

Save your settings and click on "Return to Account Settings".

I suggest you complete the Billing and Shipping Profiles because it will save you a lot of time later. This enables you to order, ship books and proofs at cost when the completed books are done, with a minimum of hassle.

The My Account page is where you can manage your account information in the future.

Now, you are ready to:

Create a book.

Log into your CreateSpace account.

Go to My Account and then Member Dashboard. Click on "Add New Title".

Start Your New Project by adding the name of the book, which you can change at any time before publication. Check the Paperback option and choose a setup process. I suggest you use the "Guided" wizard because it is much easier and less time consuming to make changes. I guarantee you will make changes.

Click the "Get Started button". This will take you through four steps and their sub-steps.

- Title
- Interior
- Cover
- Complete Setup

Title Information

The wizard will have already filled in the title from a previous step, but you can change it if you like, until you are ready to submit for review.

The primary author is your name or a pen name if you wish. You can have more than one author under the same CreateSpace account. If you have more than one author you can put it under "Add Contributors" in a box below.

"Description" is the description that will appear in the CreateSpace store and will also appear inside Amazon as you want it to appear in their catalog.

Subtitle is extremely important. This is where you tell what the book is all about. You should include key words and phrases to make the book more search engine friendly.

Volume number is for multi-volume projects and help readers to identify where they are in the series.

When you are happy with the title information, press and save the "Continue" button at the bottom. It brings you to choosing an ISBN.

ISBN

ISBN is the International Standard Book Number that uniquely identifies a book. In the United States they are issued by a private company, RR Bowker. A single number costs as much as $125.

CreateSpace offers four options for getting an ISBN.

Choose the first option. It gives you the number for free and opens every channel for distribution that CreateSpace offers. The only small downside to this choice is that it will show CreateSpace as the publisher. The other options should be avoided unless you know exactly what you are doing. They do give you complete control over the book's imprint and allows you to print your book with other printers. But, you cannot change the title.

Once a number is assigned to your book, it cannot be changed after you submit the book for review.

Copy the ISBN to include it on your copyright page. It will help categorize your book in libraries and bookstores.

Interior of Your Book

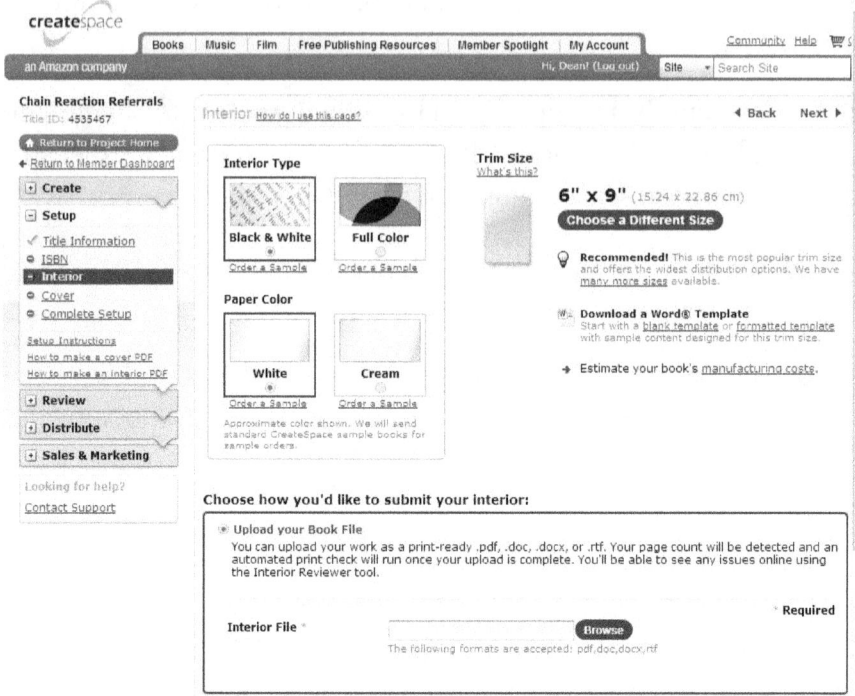

The next step is to determine the size and the color of paper and print. It is best to choose black text because graphical elements reproduce better. Color is an unnecessary expense unless it is an integral part of the content, like in a children's book. Color can double the production cost.

Trim size is the actual book size. I suggest you select the 6"x9" size because it is a clear industry standard and allows the best distribution. You may select other standard sizes if you like by clicking on the "Choose a Different Size" button. If you have a particular reason to choose a different size, you have the ability to do so. You might want to choose a larger size to accommodate pictures or graphics,

Once you have the interior qualities set, you can estimate the manufacturing costs. Click on the estimator indicated by the arrow. Now, determine the "bleed" for the pages. If you have full page photographs you will need to include a 1/8th of an inch to the top, bottom and outside edges of your pages. Most of the time you will only need no bleed where it ends before the edge of the page.

Now download a Word Template that is designed to fit the trim size you have selected. You paste (or write) your finished manuscript into the template, which you will upload to the interior file to create your book.

The final step on this page is to upload your book. I recommend you go to your book's Word template document and save it as a PDF document on your computer. The PDF will show you exactly what your book will look like and can be verified.

You could download a .docx file, but the CreateSpace program does not always interpret it properly. There will always be some errors. Create a .docx anyway as a backup.

- Save your manuscript as a PDF file to upload to the CreateSpace automatic formatter.

Automated Print Check

Push the "upload your book" button. Browse to the PDF book file on your computer. After you do this, CreateSpace will run an automated print check to look for errors and appearance.

Automated print check allows you to examine your book before you get to the digital proof stage. Look through the pages to see how they will appear when printed. If there are some problems, then go back to the original PDF file on your computer, make corrections, and upload it again. This process allows you to make corrections quickly before the human review, and saves you from having to wait a day or two for their review to finish.

Cover

Select a matte or glossy finish for your cover.

As you can see on this page you have three choices to create a cover. You can use the CreateSpace cover creator, hire your own designer to make a cover for you, or you can upload a proof-ready PDF of your cover.

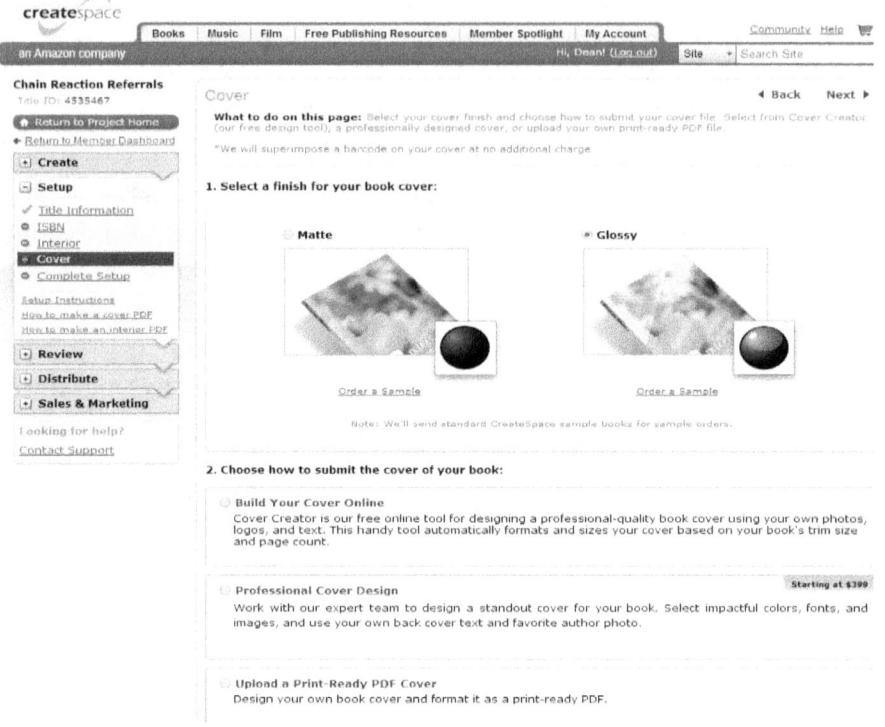

If you use the standard trim sizes you may use CreateSpace's template to put in the type on the back spine. If you don't have any special needs for your cover you could probably use the CreateSpace cover creator.

The cover creator has over 30 templates which allow you to change title, author information, and back cover details. Since you can change color schemes, fonts, and backgrounds you have a wide variety of possibilities. The cover creator adds a bar code and logo, if you have one, to the back of your cover.

If you prefer, there are numerous cover creator software packages in the $50-$100 range that will give you unlimited choices.

If you use a professional cover designer, they should have the ability to adapt the cover to CreateSpace's specifications. Look for cover designers on Elance, Fiver or Google "book cover designers".

When you use the cover creator, the back cover gives you options to put a picture of the author and a publisher's logo. There is space for you to include some testimonial pull quotes and a description of the contents of your book.

Complete Set up

This is the last step before the book is reviewed by CreateSpace humans. When you submit the book for review, the title, trimmed size, cover and any edits to your interior will be locked. CreateSpace does not do any editing. Their only concern is that it will be printed correctly.

CreateSpace also offers you a digital proof where you do not have to wait to receive the actual physical book. The digital proof allows you to view your fully-formatted book in an online personal environment. You can look at a custom-generated PDF proof that displays your interior pages side-by-side or on a single page. You can open and view the PDF on your computer or print it with your local printer.

It usually only takes about a day, sometimes less, for them to complete a review. They will notify you via email that your proof is ready. I strongly suggest you order at least one copy of the physical book. I have found this is the ultimate way to proof your book. You will almost always find typographical errors, grammar errors, or changes you want to make before you offer it to the public. Make those changes to your original manuscript and resubmit it to CreateSpace. Fortunately, it is relatively easy to make any changes you want, but it does require a review again and another few days to get it the way you want.

After you accept that proof, it takes 3-5 days for your book's information to show up on Amazon. However, it is not yet ready for sale. A few days later the description will appear in their catalog.

- CONGRATULATIONS. You are now a published author.

Review

After you have completed the final proofing step, your book is ready to be sold. Your book will appear on the sales channels that you have selected in an earlier step. On Amazon.com, books usually take 3-5 days to be listed. Your title will be immediately available on the CreateSpace eStore. It may take up to five days for your thumbnail image to appear. If you have chosen the Expanded Distribution Channels for your book. It may take anywhere from 6-8 weeks for your titles to start showing up in the distribution outlets you have selected.

At this point, you can order as many copies as you want for delivery in just a few days.

Distribution

You have already selected the distribution channels, but you want to make the book as easy to find as possible. During this distribution phase you have the opportunity to tell potential customers about your title. The description appears on your Amazon.com detail page, and may be used in other sales channels if you choose. The description can have up to 4,000 characters or about 750 words. This is another place where you want to "sell" your book. Since most people read this description before they purchase it, it is important to give the benefits your book offers.

This is where you select your BISAC category. There are dozens of categories and dozens more subcategories in which to place your book. Try to zero in on your specific category or niche. When your book goes live on Amazon you begin competition with others in your field.

You also have the opportunity to add the author's biographical information. This is a great place to tell potential readers about your expertise and how this book will solve their problem. You can expand your expertise, tell readers about your other books and generally sell yourself.

One of the other boxes in this distribution channel gives you the opportunity to label your work with keywords to make it easier for readers to shop.

Kindle or Ebook Format

CreateSpace will now give you the option to also publish an electronic version of your book. This option will send your book's interior and cover files over to KDP. They say that it will automatically convert your CreateSpace manuscript to an electronic version, although I have found that it is seldom formatted correctly for the electronic space. The reason is obvious: electronic formats range anywhere from pocket-sized cell phones to full-page electronic pads and desktop computer screens. The formatting software must take considerable license in converting any images, graphics, page breaks, styles, etc. It seldom comes out correctly.

We will talk about how to publish a Kindle electronic book in the next section.

Distribution Channels

Your Expert Book will probably not follow the same path as books made to sell primarily on the open market, but you might want to pursue all the channels anyway. For example, if your Expert Book is just for a local market, you will not select the "expanded distribution".

Amazon gives you three free standard distribution channels:

1. It will be offered on Amazon.com, which is offered to over 200 million Amazon customers.
2. Amazon Europe makes your book available to Amazon's European website which includes England, France, Italy and Spain.
3. Finally, it is offered at the CreateSpace eStore where the store orders, handles the customer service, collection of money and payment, refunds and royalties.

Expanded distribution gives you the opportunity to access a larger audience through other online retailers, bookstores, libraries, academic institutions, and other distributors within the United States. Most of these institutions purchase from wholesalers or distributors. Barnes and Noble and distributors such as Ingram are accessible this way.

Baker and Taylor offers books to libraries and academic institutions.

CreateSpace directly makes your books available to certified resellers to their wholesale website.

All the distribution options are also available on the Kindle electronic versions (see next chapter).

To become eligible for this expanded distribution, it is necessary to have an ISBN in industry standard trim sizes. Go to this distribution section in your CreateSpace account to see the details.

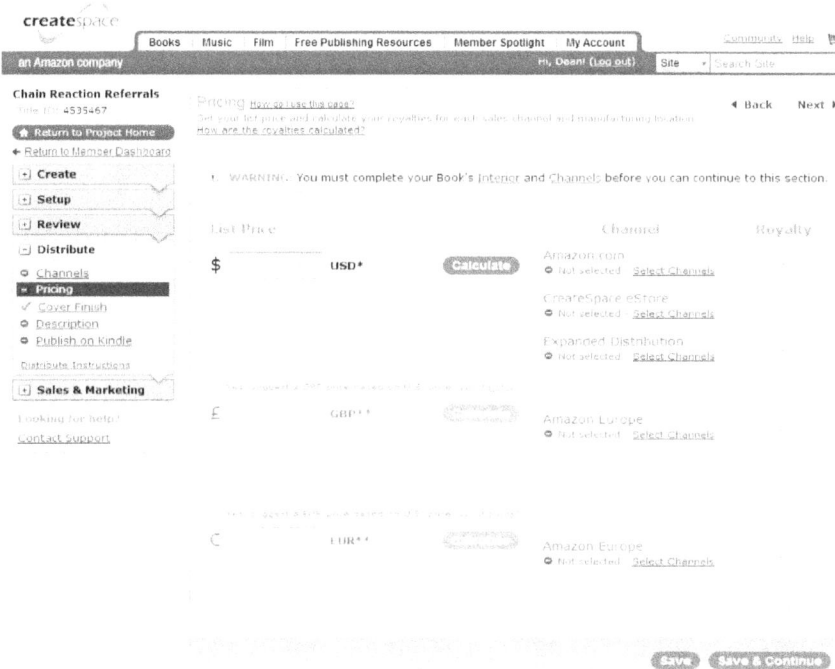

Pricing

Click on "Pricing" under "Channels" to calculate how they are paid out under the expanded distribution channels. Put in the list price of your book and it will calculate the royalties in U.S. Dollars, Pounds and Euros.

Discount codes

You have further pricing flexibility by offering discount codes though the CreateSpace store. You may want to offer incentives to book buyers for several reasons. Wholesalers or bookstores may want to order multiple copies for resale or offer a premium. Discount codes are automatically generated and are independent of titles, so a content provider of several titles may use the same code for all of his/her titles. This makes it easy to support retailers since they only need one code for multiple titles.

Codes may offer a discounted price, for example $5.00 off, or percentage discount, for example, 40% off. A title may have multiple discount codes associated with it to facilitate multiple promotional campaigns for resellers. These discount codes can be tracked to help authors monitor resale and promotional campaigns.

How to set up a discount code:

1. Log in in to your CreateSpace member account using your email address and your account password.
2. Click on the title name you wish to edit.
3. On the project homepage, click on "Channel" in the Distribute section.
4. On the Channels page, select the "discount code" under the CreateSpace eStore.
5. Click the link that reads "to create a new discount code click here". This will create a unique code that can be used across titles, or you if you have previously created code and want to apply to a new title you can skip the creating a new code.
6. To apply the code to a title, return to previous page.
7. Paste the code into the "discount" table, then set the pop-up to "discounted price and entered the dollars off or set a percentage off". Remember the discount amount was never dropped below the minimum price of the title. You can add up to three discount codes at a time.
8. To complete the process, click on the "Save changes" button.
9. Your discount code is now ready to use, and that discount you offer will be deducted on orders placed using the code.

To remove a discount, simply check the box in the Delete area of the appropriate discount, and then click Save.

Description

As part of the distribution channels, you want as many as channels for your book as possible. The description of your book falls into several categories. The book description is displayed on your books at Amazon.com's detail page and it may be used as your book's description on another sales channels. The description can have up to 4,000 characters or about 750 words. The description should focus on the book itself, describing what is in the book and benefits of reading.

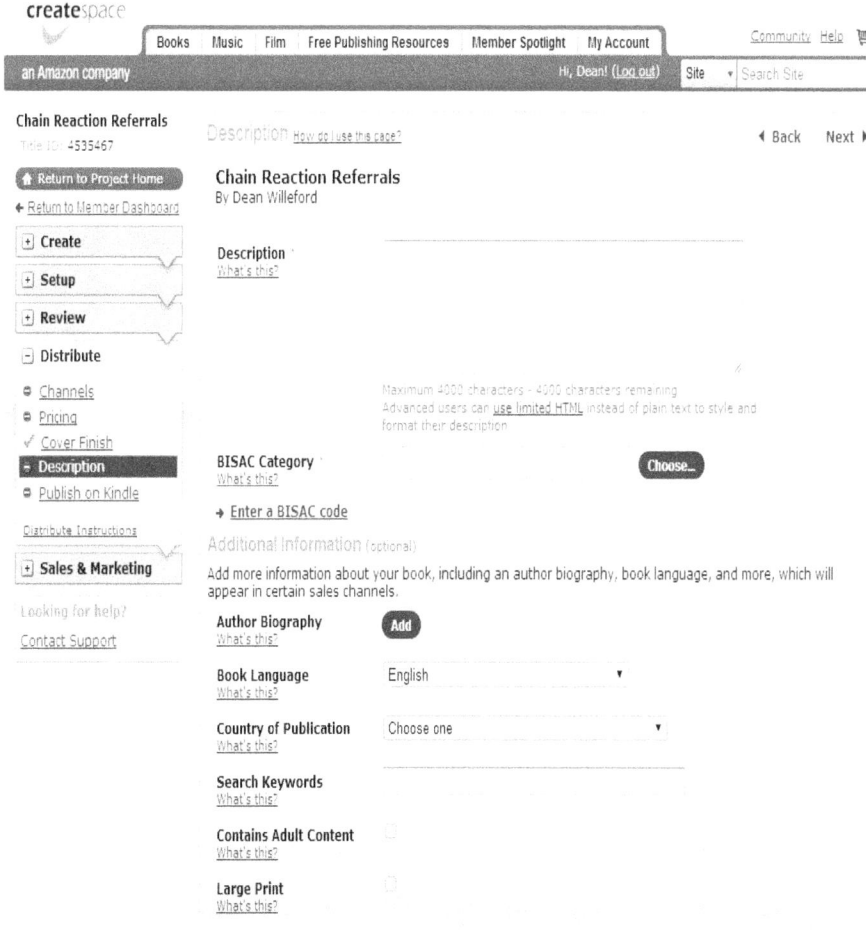

For a good examples of what should go in your description, look at other books in your category on Amazon.

Next, you need to choose a few categories used by the bookselling industry to help identify your subject matter. Choose the category that comes closest to your book. Click and choose the button for the list of categories. You're basically limited to two categories.

Author Biography

The "Author biography" tells potential readers about the author. You should include information about the author's background and qualifications, other books, publications, credentials and personal interests. This section gives you about 475 words to present yourself. For a good examples of what should go in your description, look at other books in your category on Amazon.

Next, you need to choose a few categories used by the bookselling industry to help identify your subject matter. Choose the category that comes closest to your book. Click and choose the button for the list of categories. You're basically limited to two categories.

The "Author biography" tells potential readers about the author. You should include information about the author's background and qualifications, other books, publications, credentials and personal interests. This section gives you a

Key words

This section is extremely important. Key words are those that your customers are likely to use when searching on Amazon or various search engines for your title or subject. You can use up to five key words or phrases separated by commas. You should list key words that are in your title, subtitle or in the subject of the book.

If your book contains adult content not suitable for minors under the age of 18, your book may be suppressed from some searches. Be sure to check the adult content box if it applies to your book.

Set the publication date. If you do not, it will default to the date the book is approved for sale. Once the date is set, it cannot be changed when ready for sale.

Ready to Sell

At this point you are ready to publish. You should have ordered a physical copy and are waiting for the proof to arrive in the mail. This usually takes about a week in the United States. As an added precaution, I would advise you to wait for the physical book, and proof it once more. After you have done that, make any last minute edits, changes and corrections, and order another proof to finalize before the introduction on Amazon. I know this seems like overkill, but you will be surprised at the things you will find in proofing the actual physical book.

Other Solutions

We have spent considerable time looking at CreateSpace for on demand physical books, because it is the biggest and has the support and coordination of Amazon, but there are other options in the physical book space.

There is LULU Books.com, Diggypod Inc., Lighting Source (Ingram's Print on Demand), PubIt, Xlibris and numerous other self-publishers and vanity press companies.

One of the most interesting new technologies is Espresso Book Machine (EBM). EBM makes a paperback book in minutes, at the point of need. These machines are being placed in bookstores, libraries and other retailers. Through the EspressoNet digital catalog, you can order a book online or onsite and have the book produced in minutes. For self-publishers this means readers could download your book to their catalog and have the book available wherever the machine exists. It means no inventory, any quantity and immediate pick up.

Chapter 6

Ebooks and Kindle

You probably want to publish your book as an ebook, on Amazon Kindle Direct Publishing (KDP). By clicking on the KDP option, CreateSpace will carry over your book cover and many of the details about your book to Kindle. It offers the opportunity to transfer your book interior files also. But since CreateSpace is in a PDF format, it will not translate to the electronic format well. Do not try this, because the formatting will look terrible in the electronic format. Go ahead and have CreateSpace Center send your book over to Kindle, but then take a look at an electronic preview in the "Previewer". Now you have an excellent idea of the things that you need to fix to make it show up in an acceptable Kindle ebook format. You will choose many of the same options as the physical book you created with CreateSpace, but several will be different because the format is different.

Format Differences: Kindle Ebooks

Reading a book on electronic formats is an entirely different experience than a physical book. The reader will not notice the difference in preparation, but the author and publisher have an entirely different set of challenges.

The ebook experience is quite different on a smartphone, various sizes of pads, or on a full size computers screen. Also, page count will change depending on the text size a reader chooses. Because the electronic format has such a wide variety of sizes it requires a different book preparation process than CreateSpace, print on demand and other forms of publication. For example, there really is no set page numbering as in a traditional book, because the different sizes require pages to adapt to the size of the device format. Your book may turn out to have 100 pages on iPad, or it might be 200 pages on an iPhone or Android screen. The book is cramped on a smartphone and Kindle, but almost totally normal on large pads, laptops and desktop computers.

Since you have already created the front matter and the back matter for your physical book it will be easy to insert this information into the electronic version.

Here are a few things you want to keep in mind before you submit your manuscript in an electronic format.

- Set your book up in Microsoft using Word's styles. The Normal Style allows you to use a consistent set of writing tools throughout your book. Go to the main Word writing tools ribbon and look for the symbol that looks like a backwards "P". Click on it. How you will see many symbols that show you where all the page elements are. Go through and remove things that shouldn't be there. There should be one at the end of each paragraph. Remove all the others except the one with the dotted line that says "Page Break". Click on the backwards "P" and all the symbols will disappear. What you have done by removing all the indents, breaks and other elements from your composition is to clean it up so it displays better in an electronic format.

- Enter a page break at the end of every chapter to prevent the text from running together. To enter a page break in Word: Click "Insert" at the top of the screen, click "Pages" and then "Page Break" from the menu. Insert where you want them. Start a new chapter on the next page.

- Use an electronic book template. The template will allow you to input all of your text and images into a format that's easily digestible by the electronic version. We suggest the Kinstant Formatter. It will give you the MOBI files that work best with Kindle. Kinstant will generate a Table of Contents based on the Style headings.

- We suggest you leave out any special formatting when going to the electronic version. Electronic versions have no page numbers, headers, bullets, footers.

- Use "serif" type fonts in a 12 to 14 point size. Don't use larger than 18 point headings. Kindle will override any fancy fonts that you may use, so it is best to use Times New Roman or Georgia fonts to come closest to what you will see on the screens.

- Try to avoid extra tabs and lines.

- Try to use a block style paragraph with no indentation.

- Use "serif" type fonts in a 12 to 14 point size. Don't use larger than 18 point headings. Kindle will override any fancy fonts that you may use, so it is best to use Times New Roman or Georgia fonts to come closest to what you will see on the screen.

- Don't try to upload a PDF file to the Kindle platform. It just will not come out correctly.

- Avoid drop caps at the beginning of paragraphs.

- Grayscale works best for images, although Kindle Fire and others do display color.

We suggest you use the Kinstant formatter to convert your e-book (www.word2Kindle.com). There are others, but this one works well.

Table of Contents (TOC)

Readers want you to have a Table of Contents (TOC) that links or jumps to chapters in your book. It makes the reading experience much easier and allows the reader to find information much more quickly. There are two ways to add a table of contents, either manually or automatically.

- **Manually**. You create bookmarks throughout your book for each chapter. To insert bookmarks, you place your cursor at the beginning of a chapter or subchapter and click on Insert> bookmark. Then name the bookmarks. Go to the beginning of each chapter and type out your list of title chapters. On each one you highlight and right-click, select hyperlink, select "place in this document" and choose the bookmark that corresponds to each.

- **Automatically.** Just go to References>Table of contents> Insert Table of Contents. After you enter your contents, you can right-click anywhere in the table of contents and click "update field", it will update the table of contents for you. In the Kinstant you will create a TOC based upon heading styles. There is an option before conversion, "Add/Replace table of contents". Just check that you have a hyperlinked table of contents.

Hyperlinks

If you'd like to add links in your ebook, go to the "Insert" tab on your Word ribbon, then click "Links" and type in the text that you want linked, then highlight, right-click and select Hyperlink from the box that pops up. Be sure to include the http:// part in the beginning or it won't work. Links are extremely important in an Expert Book. They enable the reader to get to you and your website quickly and easily.

Images

Avoid pasting in images. Images should be inserted. Go to "Insert" on the Word ribbon, click "Picture", which bring up a box to select the picture you want. Click it and go to "Page Layout" to select the kind of text "wrap" you want around the images.

To edit images throughout your e-book, go to Insert>Picture and then browse to the image you want on your computer and select it.

Kindle prefers images of a resolution of at least 300 DPI. They support image formats of .gif, .bmp, and .png with sizes up to 127 kb. Photographs should be .jpg with a quality factor of 40 or higher with a minimum size of 600 x 800. Line art should be .gif with a maximum size of 500 x 600

Conversion with Kinstant

Kinstant is conversion and formatting tool that creates a MOBI file for the upload to Kindle. (http://KinstantFormatter.com)

When you convert with Kinstant, the first thing it will ask you to do is to log into your Kinstant account and upload your manuscript file. It will then upload the file and analyze it for you. The software will show you what needs to be adjusted. If necessary go back to your manuscript and make corrections. It will then ask you to upload your cover. The upload will fail unless it is at least 500 x 800. When you have your cover uploaded it will ask you to enter your title and author's name. Click on the "Generate" button to convert your file.

You will be taken to a preview option inside the Kindle publishing platform where you can view your book after you upload. I strongly recommend you review it before you upload it. You can download the free Kindle preview software that is available directly from Amazon. It will be the last download listed on the above page. After you review it and make any corrections you are ready to upload it to Amazon.

Publishing Your Ebook

Go to Amazon KDP main page. From here you log into your KDP account or create one. It just takes a few minutes to create one at the "Sign Up" button. Read through Amazon's terms of use and click the agree buttons.

Kindle Direct Publishing (KDP) now walks you through your account information so you can get paid and make many other choices about your account.

- You can get paid by direct deposit. There is no fee, you get paid more quickly and don't have to wait to accumulate over

$100 in royalties before you get paid, like you would with a paper check.

- KDP will present you with a new window where they will ask if you would like to participate in KDP Select. Enroll in KDP Select if you like the terms. There really is only one negative: You are agreeing not to make your book available in digital formats on any other electronic platform for at least 90 days. That includes selling a PDF version on your own website. There is no restriction about publishing a physical book at the same time. You can print as many physical books and distribute as many as you want to boost your "expert status". Bear in mind that the KDP Select program renews automatically, so you need to terminate your participation in the program before offering a digital format elsewhere.

  You are able to offer your book for free download for the five days, which can give your book great exposure, build a following and get reviews. In exchange, you will be paid a share of the monthly reserve fund when someone some of borrows your e-book.

After you make the KDP Select decision go through and complete all information about your book. Here are a few tips about each section similar to the CreateSpace account set.

- **Title**: fill out your exact title. If you have a subtitle use a colon (:) between the title and subtitle.

- If your book is part of a series, complete the edition and volume number.

- **Description**: you have over 4,000 characters to use to describe your book. This is an excellent place to sell readers on your book. Tell the reader what the book is about and what benefits it provides.

- **Book contributors**: This is the place to let readers know about the other people who made your book possible, like illustrators, researchers, etc. The author's name is the minimum entry.

- **Verify your publishing rights**. Public domain works are allowed, but there needs to have been significant revision to make it unique. Amazon says, "It must be a unique translation, contain annotations, unique, handcrafted additional content including study guides, literary critiques, detailed biographies, or detailed historical content, or the illustrated, including 10 or more unique illustrations relevant to the book. Your description must have a bullet list of the revisions."

  The second option says you own the rights to the material because you have personally researched, written or commissioned it to be written; in short, it is your original work.

- **Categories and keywords**: You are allowed only two categories, so choose the exact category of readers you are seeking. It is a good idea to do keyword searches to find out how potential readers are searching for your topic. These should be the terms that people are entering into Amazon to explore your topic.

- **Book cover**: This is the cover that will appear in the marketplace. If you already have an image of your book's interior file, uncheck the box that says, "the book cover inside your book". Your book cover image should have a minimum setting of at least 500 pixels wide and 800 pixels long. It should be either .jpg or .tiff file extension.

- **Digital Management Rights**: Select a digital rights management option (DMR). If you want to be sure people will have to purchase your book, enable DRM. If you want people to be able to share it without any compensation, check the second option, "Do not enable DRM".

- **Upload your book file** Now you're ready to **browse** for your book and upload your e-book file from your computer to Kindle. Click "Upload Book". During the time that Kindle is processing your book you will see a message saying "converting book file to Kindle format". I would suggest you wait until the process is finished so that you can preview your book after the conversion process. After you have reviewed the book you can then hit the "Save and Continue" button in the lower right hand corner.

- Next, you have the choice between worldwide rights and individual territories. I suggest you click on "worldwide", unless you have a specific reason to limit certain countries.

- **Royalties.** They now ask you to choose what percentage royalties you would like to have, either 35% or 70%. Of course, you would pick 70% royalties, but you need to meet the following three criteria:
    1. The work has to be an original work, not public domain work.
    2. You must sell your e-book for a price between $2.99 and $9.99.
    3. You must also pay a tiny delivery cost for each book.

There is a royalty calculator in this section for you to see what the estimated royalty would be at various book prices.

There are three groups of people who might choose the lower 35% bracket:

1. People who want to publish public domain works.
2. People who would like to create a book for lead generation purposes. The minimum price is $.99. The lower the price the more people who will tend to purchase. But remember you only get 35% of the smaller price.
3. Authors who want to publish premium products.
   You could sell your book for as much as $199, but needless to say, there will be far fewer takers at the higher prices. Some authors want their work to be perceived as having a very high value. If your book is priced at, let's say $50, when you give one away, prospective clients will perceive it as a valuable gift.

   One of the nice benefits of the Kindle book system is that you can change the price at will as long as you follow the guidelines above.

- **Pricing** your book. I suggest that you examine your competition to see how they are pricing similar works. Go to Amazon.com and type in your book's category to see other books in niche. You probably want to be competitive with those other works, unless there is something truly unique about your book that can command a higher price. Since this is an electronic version of the book it will probably be priced less than a physical copy.

  Once your book is live, you can still change your book price as long as it is not in active promotion. You will have to wait for books in the "Review or Publishing" status to be "Active" before you can change the price. Your book may be unavailable for purchase for up to 24 hours while the price change takes place.

- You have further pricing flexibility because you can create a discount code for your book and offer that discount to "special" buyers. For example, you might offer a discount code to companies or people who want to buy multiple copies of your book.

- Be sure to click "Save and Publish" at the very bottom of the page when you're ready.

- KDP authors who receive their royalty payments electronically will now be paid in full every month for their sales without waiting for a minimum threshold for the payout. This gives the author greater access to their earnings and more reliable payment schedule, 60 days after the month's royalties are earned. You can set up electronic funds transfer for your account. Simply sign in to your KDP account and under "Your royalty payments", for each applicable marketplace.

Chapter 7

Marketing Your Book

You can only hand out a limited number of books personally, although that will probably be your primary distribution method. Don't assume that "if you write, they will come", they will not unless you heavily market it. Your real goal for your Expert Book is to spread your fame, expertise and authority widely in your market.

If you do want to sell your book, there are dozens of ways to do so, but you want to focus your marketing effort on your specific market. Markets in this case can mean a number of things. For example, in real estate, it may mean a limited, geographic market like your town and city or region. It might be aimed at a specific group of people, like investors, first-time homebuyers, manufacturers, retailers, vacation home buyers or any other group that has a specific real estate need.

You can spend an unlimited amount of money on marketing your book. But you always want to keep in mind your return on investment. A book can be sold like any other product. All the suggested marketing techniques below are no cost or inexpensive ways to sell books.

25 Ways to Sell More Books

If your primary goal is to sell more books for the royalties, let's look at some of the ways to market and sell your book. But always remember your primary aim is to use the book to emphasize your expertise and capture new clients. One new client will be worth hundreds, if not thousands, of book sale royalties.

Press Kit

If you want to pursue heavily marketing your book, I strongly suggest you create a press kit that can be used in conjunction with many of the marketing ideas below.

The press kit should contain the following:

- A high quality double pocket folder with a color graphic, photography or picture of your book cover on the front.
- A business card inserted in a slot on the inside cover.
- A single sheet press release inserted on the inside left pocket. Google "Press release" for the proper format.
It should have your contact information, photography of your book cover, a large clear headline, 7 to 10 bulletin points of the important highlights or benefits of your book. You should also have your head shot photography and a short bio. Obviously you want to include book ordering information. If you are looking for promotional interviews

add above 10 sample interview questions. Create all this in color for the greatest impact.
- A short hand written note or Post it note thanking them for the opportunity to present your book.
- Any testimonials or media clippings.
- Enclose the kit in an eye catching, colored 10-13 inch envelope.

I would suggest you hand address it. In the lower left corner of the envelope write, "Requested Material Enclosed".

1. **Set up a website *dedicated* to your book**.

The website can be simple, but very powerful. It gives you the opportunity to sell the book and yourself. The website enables you to point *all* of the other promotional activities to it. The book website becomes a business where you can promote the book, your other related business and product spin offs. The site gives you an opportunity to create a list of all interested parties. The site allows you to link to Amazon for direct sales, or to bypass Amazon and offer the book as an instant PDF to readers. You can easily add a shopping cart to your website for direct sales.

Be sure to link to your regular website to and from the book site.

You probably already have a website for your professional activities. Create an additional page to promote your book and its benefits. Offer free copies in exchange for their contact information. You can then begin pursuing those new people to become your customers/clients. Be sure to include a picture of your book cover and you.

Trade ads and images with other complementary sites with links back to their website. For example, if you are a veterinarian you might put an ad on your site for a local pet supply store, and they in turn put your ad and book image on their site.

One of the website pages should be a media page, with material similar to the press kit.

2. Create an electronic version.

The most important ebook site is Kindle Direct Publishing (KDP), because it is backed by Amazon, but there is also LuLu.com and Nook Press. LuLu.com offers the same publishing services as KDP, but with a higher royalty rate, although it appears their production costs are a bit more for physical books. Pubit!, Nook Press, is an ebook self-publishing platform of the big book retailer Barnes and Noble. You can also look at Booklocker, www.booklocker.com, and eBook Shoppe, www.ebookshoppe.com.

3. Create an audio book version.

Audiobook popularity is growing rapidly, and it gives you yet another channel to spread you expert status and fame. Publish on Amazon CreateSpace, as a CD. The cost from Amazon is $4.95 for one to $2.97 in quantities of 100 or more. Amazon then gets 15% on eStore or 45% on Amazon.com. Example: @ $25.00 list price would be: Amazon's share is $8.70; your royalty is $16.30.

The Audiobook Creation Exchange (ACX) (www.acx.com) makes it easy to turn your book into audio and create a new revenue stream. ACX connects authors with professional audio producers to create audiobooks.

If your budget will not allow it, you could even use Audacity to create your own audiobook. The software is free at http://audity.sourceforge.net. You will need a headset with microphone ($20-$25), a computer, and a program like LAME to save your mp3 files.

Audible.com is also an Amazon company that offers downloads of books to iPhones, Androids, Kindle Fires and Windows Phones and over 500 mp3 players.

iTunes.com also offers the ability to sell your audio book to those who have iPads, iPhones.

4. List on as many distribution channels as possible.

See your CreateSpace account under Distribution Channels.

Smashwords, Inc. distributes your ebook to the Apple iBookstore, Barnes & Noble, Sony Reader Store, Kobo, the Diesel eBook Store, Baker & Taylor's Bilo and Axis360 (libraries). Speedy Publishing.com has a wonderful list of distribution options.

5. Social media

Get your book on as many appropriate social media sites as possible. There are dozens of social media platforms to connect with readers. Facebook.com is good for fans and friends. Twitter.com is great for quick announcements and updates. If you already have social media accounts, include the book in your communications with members.

LinkedIn.com gives the ability to put your book into your profile and communicate with all your network and indirectly to millions of others. You can join specialist groups, like Small Business Consultants, Real Estate Networking, Executives & Business Leaders, Directors of Business Development, or a thousand others.

You also can create your own group. Your own group could incorporate the title or subtitle of your book, a geographic area, a specific industry segment, or your name. For example, a group name might be Dean Willeford's San Francisco Online Marketers The point is to zero in a specific market for your services/products.

YouTube.com lets you create a series of 5 to 10 short videos that you can post to Youtube.com or Vimeo.com. It is free and has worldwide audiences of millions of people. The videos can be 2 to 5 minutes long and talk about various aspects or chapters of your book. Of course, you put a call to action at the end of the video to contact you, or to purchase your book.

6. Email.

Add your book title and subtitle to your signature on all email. Type "email signature" in any of the email browsers and they will tell you how to add that information to every email you send.

7. Build a blog.

Build a blog about the subject of your book, or participate in forums about your industry.

8. Enroll in KDP Select.

KDP requires your book be exclusively posted on Amazon, so it limits the distribution on the other digital platforms. But you can cancel after 90 days, post and distribute on other e-book programs. The Select program gives you the largest free distribution and you can get paid for the books that are borrowed from Amazon.

When you enroll your title in KDP Select, your title will be included in Kindle Unlimited, which allow reader to read over 600,000 titles. When readers read past 10%, you will earn a share of the KDP Select monthly global fund. See Amazon KDP Select program for all the details.

9. Create an account on Goodreads .com .

You can link your books to your profile page and participate in the book giveaway programs to further enhance your reputation expertise.

10. Reviews

Get positive reviews, especially on Amazon. Good reviews help tremendously in getting book sales. The more sales you have the more you move up the rankings in your book category. Once you begin to get reviews in hand you can use them on other marketing materials.

11. Keywords

Spend some time to discover the best keywords for your book material. Both Google and Amazon have tools that let you discover the most popular keywords. Use those keywords on any search engines, websites, and blogs.

12. Paid adverting

Like any other product, you can purchase advertising both online and offline. Advertising works best in local publications or niche magazines.

One of the ad mediums for promoting books on radio and television shows is to run a magazine ad in the Radio Television Interview Report produced by Steve Harrison at Bradley Communications (see Resources). This publication goes to thousands of producers and stations looking for interview topics.

13. Bulk and premium sales.

Depending on the kind of Expert Book you create, there may be opportunities to sell your book in bulk to organizations. Companies may want to give away your book as a premium for the purchase of their related product/service. Your book might fit the needs of a company to give away to their internal staff, or as a training piece.

14. Amazon Author pages.

Author pages list every other book or product that you have published on Amazon.com. More importantly, for Expert Book purposes, it allows you to also list awards and other positive comments about your book and other interesting promotional information that come up customers might like to see

15. Write more books.

Write more books that are related to your subject, each with a little different angle. You can begin to build a following.

16. Translate the book into other languages, if appropriate.

17. Hire a literary agent or publicity agent

18. Build a Mailing list.

Create a list of former customers, prospects, former contacts, and current vendors. Purchase a list of specific targets. Set up an email campaign to both email or "snail mail" and expose your book to them. Send a press release to all appropriate local and national interested parties, specialty magazines, newsletters and newspapers.

19. Create lucrative spin-offs.

Many books have other products and services that expand the information in a book, including coaching programs, audio/video products, seminars, even affiliate commissions from products suggested in your book. Use Udemy.com and similar site to sell the book and spin off products.

20. Speaking.

Use your book as a basis for paid speaking engagements and sell the book at the "back of the room" after speaking events.

21. Press Releases.

Press Release have the advantage of reaching a large number of people for a relative low cost. You get to appear in front of the audience the publication already has. Create press releases and distribute in your local market or niche magazines. If they publish it, use the clipping in your other marketing materials.

A press release should be formatted like this:

```
                    PRESS RELEASE TEMPLATE
                          AP STYLE
                          Letterhead
                         Company Logo
NEWS RELEASE (in bold)                        CONTACT INFO
                                              NAME & TITLE
    February 19, 2013                         PHONE NO.
                                              EMAIL
  FOR IMMEDIATE RELEASE

                         Title/Headline
                            Subhead
                           - space -
CITY, STATE (in all caps) - First paragraph text. Answer or address the "5 Ws"
(who, what, where, when, why it's important). blah blah blah blah blah blah blah
blah blah blah blah blah blah. More details. Supplemental information. blah blah
blah blah blah blah blah blah blah blah blah blah maybe a quotation. Blah blah blah
blah blah blah blah blah blah blah blah.

          Boilerplate, aka company bio, mission, and contact info as the last thing.

                    -  # # # # # # #  -   (use pound signs to signal the end of the press release)
                         - more -         (use this if the release continues onto 2nd page)
```

PressCable (see Resources) has a service that will distribute your press releases to hundreds of news sites. This has the added advantage of creating better ranking on your website and much more traffic to look at your offering.

SpeedyPublishing also has an inexpensive press release program aimed at specifically promoting books

22. Local Book Stores.

Go to your local stores and offer it for them to retail it for you. You will have to wholesale it to the store for at least 40% off the retail price. See if you can set up a book signing in the store.

23. Listmania!

Listmania is an Amazon marketing tool that allows authors to create a list of products and books. Create a list of books in your niche that become a reference resource for interested parties. Include your works in the list. Go to Amazon.com and type in Listmania to create.

24. Hyperlink.

Set up links from your regular website to your dedicated book website and to the Amazon and other sales pages. Put links in your book to other products and services you offer.

25. Radio and TV Interviews.

While you are promoting yourself and your business refer to your book, and the benefits of reading it. Offer it free in exchange for contact information. "The first 20 people who contact my office will receive a free copy." You can put an offer in any kind of advertising.

Alex Carroll has a great system to mount a radio and television interview campaign for Radio Publicity at mailto:http://www.webmarketingmagic.com/app/aftrack.asp?afid

He has appeared on over 1300 shows and received millions of dollars of free book publicity. He has taught over 10,000 authors and product promoters how to get free radio interviews. If you are looking for free publicity, then look no further than Mr. Carroll's program.

Dan Janal at http://www.EditorLeads.com has a service where he matches reporters looking for good quote on your topic to you. He routinely get authors featured in publications like The New York Times, USA Today, Wall Street Journal, Business Week, Cosmopolitan, Women's World, etc. in hundreds of niche markets.

Chapter 8

Conclusion

This book is not meant to give you a complete overview of the self-publishing industry, but to get you excited about the potential benefits of becoming a published expert author. But, you can create an Expert Book with Amazon /CreateSpace using only the information in this book.

The biggest obstacle to becoming a published author is usually procrastination and fear that the publishing process can be overwhelming. Moving through the process quickly eliminates those obstacles. A coaching publisher, such as ExpertPublisher.com, can be a tremendous help in realizing your dream.

There are numerous people and companies on the Internet who can help you through the publishing process. Expert Publisher takes a direct, hands-on, personal approach that is aimed to get your book done quickly, hold you to a schedule, so you can begin using your book to attract more business quickly.

Don't believe the claims of writing *and* publishing a book over the weekend, or in one week; it simply takes more time to create more than a "pamphlet" on your expertise.

Writing an Expert Book is well worth the time and investment in the short term for you to realize years of benefits. Start today and in less than 60 days you will be congratulating yourself.

If you would like the author to come speak to your event or group about writing a book, give me a call at (775) 827-1775.

I sincerely wish you the best of luck in creating your Expert Book. If you found this book helpful, write and let know at ConsultwithPro@yahoo.com.

Resources

Books

The Complete Guide to Self-Publishing, by Marilyn Ross and Sue Collier, F&W Publications Inc., Cincinnati, OH

Guerrilla Marketing for Writers: 100 Weapons to Help Sell Your Work, by Jay Conrad Levinson, Writer's Digest Books, Cincinnati, OH. : 2000

The Self-Publishing Manual: How to Write, Print and Sell Your Own Book, by Dan Poynter, Para Publishing, Santa Barbara, CA : 2007

Start Your Own Self-Publishing Business, Entrepreneur Magazine, by Cheryl Kimball, 2012

Print-On-Demand Book Publishing: A New Approach to Printing and Marketing Books for Publishers and Self-Publishing Authors, by Morris Rosenthal, Foner Books, 2008

ReferralsAnd...Recommendations,Introductions, Endorsements, Testimonials, Reviews, and Word of Mouth, by Dean Willeford, Xpert Publisher, Reno, Nevada, 2014

Words that Sell, by Richard Bayan, Contemporary Books, Chicago, Illinois, 1984

Consultants

www.ExpertPublisher.com

Covers

www.mybookcover.com

www.Createspace.com

Cover Design

www.Elance.com

www.Fiver.com

www.99Design.com

Opus 1 Design, Pam Terry, P.O. Box 3653, Beverly Hills, CA 90035. www.opus1design.com

1106 Design.com. , Michele De Filippo

E-Publishers

Bookface Technologies, www.bookface.com

Booklocker, www.booklocker.com

eBook Shoppe, www.ebooklocker.com

Kindle Direct Publishing, www.KDP.com

ISBN and SAN Provider

R.R. Bowker, www.bowker.com

Print on Demand

CreateSpace, www.createspace.com

Lulu, www.lulu.com

PubIt, www.barnesandnoble.com

Xlibris, www.xlibris.com

Publicity

Press Releases, http://www.SpeedyPublishing.com

Press Releases, http://www.PressCable.com

Steve Harrison, Bradley Communications Corp.

http://www.RadioTelevisionInterviewReport.com

http://www.The PublicitySummit.com

Alex Carroll, free radio interviews

http://www.RadioPublicity.com

Dan Janal, publications publicity

http://www.EditorLead.com

Wholesalers

Baker and Taylor, www.btol.com, (800) 775-1800

Ingram Book Company, www.ingrambook.com, (615) 793-5000

(KDP, 90, 100
"go to", 19
"go to", *28, 39*
About the Author, *7, 13, 24, 25, 50, 59*
ACX, 100
ADP, *85*
Amazon, *11, 13, 20, 22, 24, 27, 29, 50, 52, 53, 54, 55, 56, 58, 60, 63, 65, 66, 69, 71, 76, 77, 78, 81, 82, 83, 85, 90, 92, 94, 99, 100, 102, 103, 106, 108*
audio book, 100, 101
Author Biography, 82
authority, *13, 15, 16, 19, 20, 21, 24, 25, 28, 39, 40, 51, 53, 97*
Authority, *28*
Automated Print Check, 73
avatar, *32, 44, 53*
back cover, *24, 49, 50, 55, 74, 75*
Baker and Taylor, 78, 112
Bar code, *50*
Barnes & Noble, *20, 101*
Book Description, 63
Bowker's, 67
call to action, *24, 48, 55, 102*
Call to Action, *61*
Career Builder, *25*
Complete Set up, 75
Conversion, 9, 89
Copyright, *50, 62*
Cover, *8, 10, 50, 54, 55, 70, 73, 111*
cover creator, *55, 74, 75*
Create Space Account, 68
CreateSpace, *9, 27, 55, 57, 58, 63, 65, 66, 68, 69, 70, 71, 73, 74, 75, 76, 77, 78, 79, 80, 83, 85, 86, 91, 100, 101, 108, 111*
credibility, *16, 20, 24, 25, 26, 59, 60, 61*
Description, 81
Disclaimer Liability Page, *60*
Discount codes, 79
Distribution, 9, 15, 76, 78, 101
docx file, 73
Editing, *8, 15, 47*
enhanced" resume, *25*
Espresso Book Machine (EBM)., 83
Expert Book, *1, 5, 7, 8, 9, 15, 16, 17, 43, 49, 51, 57, 59, 97, 103, 108*
Facebook, *25*, 101
Format, 9, *77, 86*
geo-specific title, *23*
go to, *21, 25, 28, 31, 39, 55, 61, 62, 63, 73, 89*
Goodreads, 102
Grayscale, 88
Hyperlinks, 89

Images, 55, 61, 89
interior, *50, 59, 72, 75, 77, 85, 92*
Interior of Your Book, 72
Interview, *46*
introduction, *21, 22, 23, 50, 57, 61, 62, 83*
ISBN, *10, 50, 55, 59, 66, 71, 79, 111*
iTunes, *20*
KDP, *77, 90, 91, 95, 100, 102, 111*
KDP Select, 91, 102
key words, *52, 53, 63, 65, 71, 82*
Key words, 52, 82
keywords, 77, 92, 103
Kindle, *9, 27, 56, 57, 65, 77, 79, 85, 86, 87, 88, 89, 90, 93, 94, 100, 111*
Kinstant, 9, 87, 88, 89, 90
Lifetime Customer Value (LCV), *31, 33*
LinkedIn, 14, 25, 101
Look Inside, *8, 56*
LULU Books, 83
manuscript, *15, 43, 46, 47, 48, 50, 65, 73, 75, 77, 86, 90*
Manuscript, *8, 49*
Marketing, *7, 9, 13, 15, 26, 31, 34, 35, 36, 97, 110*
me too, *36, 37*
Media, *7, 27*
Outline, *45*
PDF, *65, 73, 74, 75, 85, 88, 91, 99*
Price, *8, 38, 51, 57*
Pricing, *57, 79, 94*
PubIt,, 83
public domain works, *58, 94*
reviews, *60, 91, 102*
royalties, *16, 26, 27, 69, 78, 79, 90, 93, 95, 98*
Royalties, *26*
royalty, *16, 19, 57, 58, 69, 93, 95, 100*
Smashwords, Inc, 101
Speed Writing, *44*
spin off, *28, 104*
Structure, *60*
subtitle, *49, 50, 51, 52, 59, 82, 91, 102*
Table of Contents, *7, 8, 49, 51, 56, 61, 87, 88, 89*
Target and Theme, *44*
the best deal, *38*
the should asked questions, *46*
title, *11, 23, 32, 49, 51, 52, 53, 54, 55, 56, 59, 63, 65, 66, 70, 71, 74, 75, 76, 80, 82, 88, 90, 91, 102*
TOC, *56, 88, 89*
Transcription, *8, 47*
Trim size, 72
ultimate business card, *20, 22*

Ultimate Business Card, *7*
Unique Signature Marketing Position, *31*, *36*
USMP, *31*, *35*, *36*, *37*, *38*, *39*, *40*
Word's styles, 86
Xlibris, 83
YouTube.com, 101

Notes

Notes

www.ingramcontent.com/pod-product-compliance
Lightning Source LLC
Chambersburg PA
CBHW051548170526
45165CB00002B/929